I went forward with Arne a few yards behind me. 'Good luck,'said Joachim. We had calculated that the Germans would have laid mine-fields to protect the factory. If we were unlucky enough to come upon a mine, then not more than two of us would go in the first round . . .

We went right up to the gate and with the help of cutters which Arne had brought with him it was a matter of seconds to cut through a thin iron chain which barred the way to one of the most important military objectives in Eu

Also in Fontana

KNUT HAUKELID

Skis Against the Atom

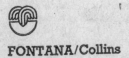

FONTANA/Collins

First published by William Kimber 1954
This revised edition first published by Fontana Books 1973
Second Impression March 1973

© in this revised edition Knut Haukelid 1973

Printed in Great Britain
Collins Clear-Type Press London and Glasgow

CONTENTS

INTRODUCTION

I am glad to write for my friend Knut Haukelid an introduction to this enthralling story of high adventure on military duty so as to give the background to the operations which this book so vividly describes, and to show how they fitted in to the wider picture of 'Resistance'. I hope too it will enable the reader to have a fuller appreciation and understanding of the remarkable exploits of a small and devoted group of Norwegian soldiers.

The operations were organised and directed by the Special Operations Executive (S.O.E.)[1] in accordance with its charter of formation by the War Cabinet in August 1940. This charged it with the conduct of subversive warfare of all kinds against the enemy, with particular reference to action in those occupied territories whose potentialities in man-power, raw materials, industrial resources, and production of war material had fallen completely into Germany's hands; assets which the Germans were not slow in exploiting. Their plans had been laid before the war began; thus it was that as each European country in turn fell under German domination, so were the experts despatched in vast numbers from Germany to link to the German war effort the wealth and productivity of the conquered lands. But there was one factor which Germany had overlooked – the undefeated spirit of thousands and thousands of men and women, temporarily overwhelmed by military defeat and disaster, but burning to continue the fight if only they could be given the means, i.e. direction, weapons and training, and told what to do. This was clearly the most fruitful field for S.O.E.

S.O.E. started, as it were, from scratch, while Germany's counterpart, including the Gestapo, had already been operating for some years, in war and in peace. The lee-way was tre-

[1] Personnel of S.O.E. while on operations were referred to as 'Special Forces' for security reasons, but the two terms are for practical purposes synonymous. I have used both according to which best fits the circumstance.

mendous, but it was clear to us that if our efficiency, methods, determination, research and development could eventually equal those of the Germans, the scales would in time, through this factor of patriotism, be weighted heavily in our favour. If we could surpass them in design, in cunning, in surprise, in boldness, then the fruit of our labours might begin to show effect in time to have some influence on the war. But many bitter and hard experiences lay ahead, of individual suffering, of grievous set-backs to our plans through error or betrayal or lack of physical resources, particularly aircraft, before we could feel that at last we had stretched our enemy to breaking point and were free to range both occupied Europe and Asia almost at will without serious hindrance from German or Japanese.

From its beginning the operational side of S.O.E., as distinct from its training branch, its supply department, its research and development branches, its financial and security branches, and so forth, was organised on the 'country-section basis'; for example, a Norwegian section, a section for Greece and Crete (at S.O.E.'s Middle East H.Q.), a Burma section (at S.O.E.'s Far Eastern H.Q.), each of whose responsibility was to encourage, develop and control subversive warfare and resistance in its relevant country, and also to find the recruits, to arrange their training with the Training Branch, and to look after them when trained. All our personnel were volunteers, whether British or Allied, men or women, whether serving at headquarters or 'in the field', or alternating from one to the other. They drew the pay of their rank whatever duty they were engaged upon, plus parachute pay if they had qualified for it as in the other services. We had one privilege: all British signallers parachuted into enemy-held territory were given the minimum rank of corporal.

Colonel J. S. Wilson was transferred on 1st January, 1942 from the Training Branch to the more exacting role of head of the Norwegian Section, when its great potentialities were becoming clear. It is of interest that the necessarily extensive and complicated programme of training for S.O.E. personnel, drawn up by Colonel Wilson in 1940 before there was a single recruit, remained basically unchanged throughout the war, and was used at home, in the Middle East and Italy, and even the Far East for native personnel; a remarkable example of imagination and foresight.

The men operating under him were Norwegians seconded to S.O.E. by the Norwegian Government in Great Britain for special service in their own country, at first very few in number but increasing as the war went on and as new fields for exploitation appeared. They were organised in what was known as the 'Linge Company', and is still historically referred to as such, in honour of their first commander, Captain Linge, who was killed in action in Norway in 1942. The men of this company were maintained permanently, were trained in Special Forces, and based in the Highlands of Scotland where the terrain as nearly as possible resembled that of their own country, and where ski-ing training could be carried out for long periods of the year. As each operation was decided upon, men were drawn from the company and despatched to carry it out, after any additional training that the particular task might necessitate. When the task was completed they were brought back to the United Kingdom by devious routes and rejoined their company, or in some cases, as with Knut Haukelid, ordered to remain in Norway for some freshly-specified task.

The same principle of organisation ran throughout all the country sections of S.O.E., except that in most of the other sections, excluding the Danish, Dutch, Belgian and Polish, a high proportion of the personnel infiltrated were British, particularly in the sections dealing with France, with the Balkans and Greece, and in the Far East where the personnel were almost entirely British and where it was very much a matter of British leadership. In Italy too, after the Italian Armistice, it was largely British officers and N.C.O.'s who were parachuted behind the German lines to organise, train and equip the Italian partisans and lead them in battle. It was a question of what was required and what was available.

Obviously for Norway it was essential to use only Norwegians; a British person parachuted into Norway, however well he spoke the language and knew the country, would at once be recognised as a stranger and would arouse intense interest and speculation, which would soon have got to the ears of the Germans. There are few Englishmen, moreover, who could have survived the physical hardships endured by Knut Haukelid and his companions – the inadequate food for weeks on end, the intense cold, the long journeys on skis by night and day. Fortunately there were enough Norwegian volunteers for our needs.

It was clear to us from the earliest days that maximum results could only be achieved if S.O.E. had the confidence not only of the limited foreign personnel serving in it, but also the support of the mass of the peoples in the territories where it was carrying out its day-to-day activities. And this could only be achieved if, where there was a *de jure* government in existence, although only in exile, the peoples could know that our actions, and theirs in concert with us, had the general approval of their government. For, at the lowest estimate, these actions would affect their daily lives, in such ways as intensified restrictive measures by the enemy, the imprisonment and execution as reprisals on innocent inhabitants, and on the highest plane affect their whole post-war position in international politics. Suffice it to say that as far as the Norwegian Government in England was concerned we had by 1942 established a good working relationship and this fact was due largely to the work of Colonel Wilson.

And so we come to Knut Haukelid's story.

It is fortunate for us that among the participants in these epic operations was one who can so vividly and yet objectively set out the story. Knut Haukelid has also the ability to turn his ever-active mind to the wider aspects of his country's secret war against the oppressor, and of the feelings and reaction of his people in these grievous but stirring years during which many nations regained their soul. Immediately after the German surrender I spent a short week in Norway, concerned with the recovery of our stores and wireless sets for use in the Far East, the recording of operations, the tracing of those who had actively helped us at the risk of their lives, and the investigation of Gestapo counter-measures that had been employed against us. I spent two days with Knut in the Rjukan valley, a ravine so deep and precipitous that in winter the sun never touches its depths, and the workers must be taken up by the cable railway to get their daily ration of sunlight. It looked even grimmer than in the aerial photographs which were all I knew of it before.

Knut is first and foremost a hunter, a man who knows and loves the wild, who is part of it, whose every sense is observant; next he is a philosopher, a man who has seen all sides of life including the experience of seven years in America, and who has come by his own experience to a sense of values reminiscent of the Greek philosophers. Thirdly and lastly, he is a man of action who faces directly any situation that comes to him, with the confidence that there must be a solution if rationality has any meaning, and that he will find it. Warm-hearted, cool-headed, yet gay, there is no better combination in peace or war.

Knut Haukelid's story divides itself into three periods, each of a slightly different character – the period leading up to and including the attack on the high-concentration (heavy water) plant at Vemork; that from 28th February, 1943 until 20th February, 1944 when he sank the ferry steamer *Hydro* on the Tinnsjö; and from then until 7th May, 1945 when the 57,000 semi-trained and semi-armed men of the secret Norwegian Home Forces took over the control of their country from the 365,000 armed German forces.

It was known in the United Kingdom in May 1940 that Germany had ordered Norsk Hydro to increase the production of heavy water (deuterium oxide) at Vemork to 3,000 lb. a year as a basic requirement in her attempts to produce the atom bomb. At the beginning of 1942 Germany demanded a further increase up to 10,000 lb. This demand afforded additional evidence of the enemy's extreme interest in the product. Immediate reference was made by the War Cabinet to S.O.E. in the hope that we might have some contacts in this activity. It so happened that, of the Norwegians under a Special Forces officer who had brilliantly captured and brought the coastal steamer *Galtesund* from Norway to Aberdeen, was one Einar Skinnarland who had an intimate knowledge of the neighbourhood of Vemork and was in touch with some of the Norsk Hydro engineers. He was given a hurried training and precise instructions and dropped back home by parachute on 28th March, 1942. This was eleven days after he had landed in Aberdeen from the *Galtesund*, and before the 'leave' he had taken from his work had expired. Thus his absence was not noticed and his visit to England remained a secret. As a further step, the 'Grouse' party of four men was also formed, ready to be dropped on to Hardanger Vidda during April 1942, but weather prevented the operation from being flown before diminishing hours of darkness put an end to all night operations to Norway till autumn should come. It was not, therefore, until 19th October, 1942, when the long nights had returned, that the R.A.F. were able to drop the party after two previous attempts had been foiled by cloud. It is noteworthy that the parachuting of Einar Skinnarland back to Norway was only the second operation that the R.A.F. had been able to carry out in Norway on behalf of Special Forces. To say the least, Norway is not suited to air operations. Possible dropping grounds are few and of very small area, mountains are thickly clustered, precipitous and angry: the broken countryside throws up air-pockets and atmospheric currents. Weather conditions on both sides of the North Sea are seldom the same, and in the autumn of 1942 were generally vile.

A raid by regular forces was being prepared for a glider-borne attack against Vemork. S.O.E. did all they could to help. Skinnarland's information was precise, but it had to be transmitted in a roundabout way through Oslo, and frequently through more distant places. There was thus a sigh of relief when the Grouse party wireless signals were heard on 9th November. The heavy snowstorms had affected their W/T set and accumulator, and the gales continually tore down their aerial, but the receiving station in England was keeping a twenty-four-hour watch. One of the messages raised our suspicions that the station had been captured, as the rate and style of sending were abnormal, but check messages disproved this. Knut Haukelid gives the reason when he says: 'Knut Haugland had been sitting at his wireless set for weeks, his fingers growing stiff and numb on the keys as the weather worsened.'

The glider-borne attack met bad weather and the gliders crashed. The Grouse leader wrote in his diary: 'London's radio message about the glider disaster was a hard blow. It was sad and bitter, especially as the weather in our part of the country improved during the following days. But we were happy to hear that another attempt would be made in the next moon period.' Immediately the news of the disaster to the glider operation became known, S.O.E. requested permission of the Chiefs of Staff to attempt the operation, as we felt there was a possibility of success by using clandestine methods. Instructions were received to proceed, so the 'Gunnerside' party was formed and its training started.

With Professor Tronstad, the Norwegian scientist, as adviser, this training was carried out by British officers, who were also responsible for the complete planning and equipping of the party. It was not by chance, to quote from Haukelid's story, that 'Joachim had taken care to bring with him from England a large pair of wire-cutters which could go through three-quarters of an inch of iron like butter'. Our technical services tried to foresee every possible necessity and provide the necessary tools and training; a model of the special concentration plant was meticulously prepared, as for other industrial targets. After months of disappointment and anxiety on account of the bad weather the Gunnerside attack party was eventually parachuted with six containers of arms, explosives, clothing and food stores, and five packages of skis, toboggan, etc. They carried out their operation according to the alternative plan with great courage, resourcefulness and success.

The second period covered by Knut Haukelid was of a different character since his primary duty was to organise Resistance in his area. It culminated, however, in the sinking of the ferry-steamer carrying off the whole stock of heavy water to Germany.

The British High Command had ruled that everything possible should be done to destroy these stocks of heavy water in transit. Since Haukelid's plan inevitably involved the loss of civilian lives, the previous approval of the Norwegian Government, was obtained under the gentleman's agreement between S.O.E. and the Norwegian Government in London, before the final message was sent to Haukelid approving the attack on the ferry-steamer.

Haukelid's account contains the same under-statements that were typical of all the many Norwegian reports rendered to S.O.E. His action was one of the most courageous, successful, and complete ever carried out in Norway. An interesting sidelight was to receive in London from Stockholm Haukelid's report of his plans and preparations, written before he had actually carried out the operation. He foretold in his plan precisely what eventually happened, even to within fifteen minutes of the actual time of the explosion.

Another small party had been sent by Special Forces to

proceed down to Skien on the coast to act as a long-stop in the event of Haukelid being unable to interrupt the convoy. Later this party complained that they had been waiting with all their preparations made but that the ball had been taken by the wicket-keeper.

In his third period of little over a year Haukelid returned to his duty of organising Resistance and was also concerned in the protective measures which were taken to ensure that the Germans did not in the final stages of the war indulge in any of the scorched-earth policy which they had pursued in withdrawing from north Norway in November 1944.

S.O.E. in conjunction with Resistance (or secret Home Forces) Headquarters in Oslo had drawn up alternative plans to be put into operation to suit the particular circumstances that might arise, as the safeguarding of Norway's industries was regarded as of considerable importance. Professor Tronstad had again acted as adviser, as he was a leading industrial chemist. His untimely and unnecessary death was greatly regretted by his British friends and comrades. It occurred on the one single occasion when neither of his bodyguards, Einar Skinnarland and Captain Norman Lind, were with him, having been sent off on different emergencies. Such is war. The only occasion when there was any disagreement between Tronstad and the Norwegian Section of S.O.E. was in connection with his insistence, with his government's backing, that he should be dropped into Norway so as to be on the spot to see that the protective operations were properly carried out locally; in the special circumstances S.O.E. gave way.

It is not generally known that every factory and every port in Norway of any size or importance was covered, some by the local Home Forces and the more important ones by parties trained specially in the United Kingdom. The latter were sent over and landed by Special Forces submarine-chasers from Shetland or dropped by the R.A.F. special squadrons. These submarine-chasers we owed to General William Donovan of the American O.S.S., who, with his characteristic generosity, obtained them for us when German aircraft had rendered other clandestine sea-traffic to Norway impossible.

This was a general extension of S.O.E. operations. As the Allied invasions progressed during the latter half of 1944, so that a successful conclusion of the war could be envisaged in the future, Allied policies were extended to cover the immediate post-war situation. It became highly important to prevent wholesale destruction by the Germans of economic assets that would delay the recovery of the liberated countries, and so create unemployment, distress, famine and political unrest. As in Norway, so in other countries, S.O.E. was now further charged with endeavouring to ensure that the least possible destruction of key services took place. This had special significance, for example, in north-east Italy, where the vast hydro-electric installations which have such a tremendous importance in the highly industrialised life of the country, had been prepared by the Germans for destruction – a plan which was successfully frustrated.

For all work in occupied territories, reliable and rapid communications were essential; wireless provided the best solution but had its own particular weaknesses. Clandestine wireless stations were always subject to radio location by the enemy and had constantly to change position and timings; the wireless operator's role was undoubtedly the most hazardous of all and called for special qualities, but there was never a shortage of volunteers. It is worthy of note that as the Allied invasions overran the Special Forces units in Western Europe and the Balkans, their British W/T operators, brought back to the United Kingdom for rehabilitation, volunteered as one man for service in the Far East behind the Japanese lines: within three weeks of arriving in that theatre some had already achieved their aim.

As in flying operations, so in wireless communications Norway is a problem country; mountains and atmospheric conditions presenting countless difficulties. Eventually S.O.E. was able to produce specially built sets to conquer these difficulties and provide for the particular skip distance demanded between Norway and the United Kingdom.

Apart from visits to and from Sweden, all the transport of the men concerned in Haukelid's saga, and the deliveries of equipment and stores, was done by air. And apart from special sorties with supplies flown by Colonel Balchen's special squadron of the U.S.A.A.F. in July-September 1944, all air operations to Norway were conducted by the R.A.F. As mentioned, Einar Skinnarland's return to Norway was only the second operation flown by them to that difficult country – one man and one container; Grouse was composed of four men, six containers and two packages, and, as I have written, Gunnerside of six men, six containers and five packages. In October 1944 two flights dropped the 'Sunshine' party of nine men, twenty-four containers and six packages. In all, the R.A.F. brought off thirty successful operations to supply the requirements of the activities in which Knut Haukelid was directly concerned, dropping twenty men, 516 containers and 168 packages. The biggest combined drop was on 2nd March, 1944 when they delivered to Swallow and Sunshine a hundred containers and twenty-four packages. But, again, the help accorded to Grouse-Swallow-Sunshine represented only a small percentage of the containers and packages supplied to Resistance in Norway and only an infinitesimally small percentage of Special Forces' European or world total. Every operation demanded agreement beforehand on the dropping point, the exchange of messages to establish whether the operation could or could not be undertaken on any particular night, co-operation both between S.O.E. and 38 Group R.A.F. and on the ground in Norway in the setting of beacons, showing of lights and the reception of men and materials. To 38 Group R.A.F. both S.O.E. and the Norwegian Home Forces are eternally grateful. This was not all the help rendered by the R.A.F., as Haukelid relates: 'Air photographs which we had of the area showed that there was a small wood bordering the ravine. Where trees grow a man can make his way.'

Came at long last the German surrender, and the Allies' first great task was done. Peace dawned again in many lands after years of brutish domination. The secret armies so painfully and laboriously built up by S.O.E. through the long dark years sprang to arms and played their part in the Allied plans. In France, as the Allies swept over the beaches of Normandy and over the Mediterranean shores, a hundred thousand Frenchmen, armed and equipped by the Allies and trained in their new weapons, leaped into open warfare behind the German lines, while selected groups of them played havoc behind our bridgeheads, Norwegians and Danes stopped and destroyed the convoys from the Russian north front with units called back by the Germans to bolster up their own crumbling front at home. Europe was at last in flames.

The culmination was the fruit of much labour, of a ceaseless burden of anxiety, of a continuous day-and-night battle with the Gestapo, week in week out, from year to year. But the days came at last when, night after night, aircraft streamed out from Britain, from North Africa, from Italy, from India and Ceylon, carrying arms and men to all occupied territories from Norway to the Spanish frontier, from Brest to the Balkans.

The most difficult aspect of all S.O.E. work was the need to carry out two broad tasks simultaneously, which were themselves hardly compatible, that is action, day by day and week after week, in specific attacks against selected targets in occupied countries, and at the same time the creation of secret armies, equipped, organised and trained, ready to come into action as ordered when invasion should come. Every attack carried out naturally alerted the Gestapo to added activity and increased the risks and dangers of discovery of the secret armies, but somehow it was done, not without casualties. Knut Haukelid brings out the point very clearly indeed, and also the dangers of a premature rising which were always present. Indeed, the news of the Allied landing in France spread over that country like wildfire.

General Eisenhower wrote in May 1945:

While no final assessment of the operational value of Resistance action has yet been completed, I consider that the disruption of enemy rail communications, the harassing of German road moves and the continual and increasing strain placed on German war economy and internal security services throughout Occupied Europe by the organized forces of Resistance, played a very considerable part in our complete and final victory.

No nation has a monopoly of courage; every nation has brave men. This fact both Germans and Japanese overlooked; they expected by execution and torture, by reprisal and concentration camp, to stifle all opposition and bring all peoples to their will, to work for them as slaves. Every oppressed nation gave them the lie.

Knut Haukelid discerningly remarks that there is nothing more depressing than to stand before one's enemy unarmed.

It was in the answer to the cry for arms to continue the fight that S.O.E. had its being and its fulfilment, that the peoples could fling off the yoke from their necks and fight as free men again and, though tortured and oppressed, hold up their heads in pride in the face of their enemy before victory was won – and afterwards.

1. FLYING HOME

On a cold January night in 1943 a big four-engined bomber left England for Norway, bound on a secret errand. The hum of the powerful engines rose and fell, and inside the aircraft conversation was almost impossible. For that matter, no one wanted to talk.

We sat on our parachutes and packs of equipment or silently jostled for the one tiny peephole that gave us a view over the North Sea. In a little while we should cross the Norwegian coast.

Having secured the desired place for myself I stared out until my eyes ached, and at last, beneath the starboard wing, caught a glimpse of moonlit sea breaking on a shoal.

We crossed the coast east of Kristiansand. A fishing boat flashed her lamp at us as we passed overhead, no doubt recognising the mysterious aircraft which came and went on moonlight nights. That glimpse of the surf had been like a greeting from the land, and now the boat's lamp imparted a feeling of comradeship with the first Norwegians we had met on our way home.

As was the custom of aircraft entering Norway on secret missions, we flew higher over the coastal belt and descended very rapidly farther inland. Then, so that the German radar stations should not keep track of us, we plunged right down and set our course along the valleys. There were the snows, the forests and fells which we had so sorely missed during our time in England. Never had the country been so beautiful as now. If we had lived a whole lifetime just to experience such a homecoming, we could not have asked for more.

Much had happened in the last three years, since the April days of 1940 when we first came in contact with the war. I had been in Narvik that winter, building a quay at which to unload war material for the Finns. On my way south in the spring I spent the night with a friend in Trondheim, and on the morning of 9th April we awoke to find the town already occupied by foreign troops. Collecting all the ski-ing equipment we had, we sneaked out of Trondheim with the idea of joining a Norwegian volunteer detachment. For we still hoped to throw the Germans out of the places they had occupied; after all, Oslo had held its own in the first round.

With a party of students from Trondheim, we made our escape southwards to the railway junction of Stören, thirty miles to the south. As we arrived a goods train containing iced fish arrived at the station. It was bound for Hamburg, of all places, and we immediately decided it should not reach Germany. A group of angry young men approached the station-master.

'Disconnect the fish vans. Hook on some empty carriages. We want to go to Oslo to fight.' The station master kept to his rules and regulations. 'The papers say Hamburg, you have no tickets, this is a goods train and the fish may be spoiled.'

It ended with a compromise. We hooked some more goods vans on to the train and started for Oslo. There was only one thought in our heads; Hitler and his gang should be thrown back into the sea. The train moved south through the peaceful but 'blacked-out' valleys. Other young men joined us during the journey and more and more vans were hooked on to the fish train to Hamburg. Some of the newcomers had brought their private rifles. We moved down through the peaceful Gudbrandsdal Valley without guessing that in a fortnight it would be a bloody battlefield between English and Norwegian infantry on one side, and German tanks and air-craft backed by their parachutists on the other side.

At Lillehammer all traffic had stopped. The Germans were already a mere ten miles to the south. We left the train, got hold of a bus and backtracked to a mobilisation depot at Starum on the west side of the big lake Mjösa. Here we begged them to give us weapons, but equipment was short and we were asked to go on still farther. It was from Starum that we witnessed the bombing of Elverum, though we thought at the time that the bombs were falling on Terning moor. Later came a report that the Norwegian warships *Eidsvold* and *Norge* had been sunk and that the Government had fled to Elverum. Afraid that the Government would give up the struggle, many of our boys sat down and wept.

That was nearly three years ago. Now, sitting in an aircraft, we saw our country again, and our joy was as great as our grief had been then. In the bright moonlight we could see every farm and every house we passed, while at some places people came out and peered up at the sky. A thousand feet or so was all the distance between that occupied country and the free fighting men aboard the plane. A couple of dogs could be seen running along a road. With a shock, I wondered whether the Germans had seen our movements as clearly on that April day three years ago, when we were on our way to Raufoss and columns of their aircraft were flying overhead.

We got no arms till we reached Brandbu. There we were each given a Krag rifle and some ammunition. Hvalsmoen had been bombed, and the depots had been moved north-ward. There were reports of hard fighting north of Hönefoss, where the 6th Infantry Regiment was holding the Germans. We asked an officer where we should report, and were told that if we wanted to shoot some Germans we must go south to Klekken. Those were all the orders we got. So we commandeered a lorry and set off. There was a hard tussle at Haugsbygda, east of Hönefoss, but in the end the Germans put in tanks and the whole of our front was ordered to retire. The last thing we saw was Haugsbygda in flames. We swore then that we would never give in – not even if the Germans won the war.

In those days we knew nothing of modern warfare, but thought that our knowledge of the forest country in Hade-land would enable us to deal with the Germans in that region. As it turned out the Germans did not concern them-selves with the forests at that time, being content to hold the roads and thereby gain some measure of control over the forests and mountains as well. So the fighting ended and we came home from a lost war, to a way of life that was shat-tered to fragments. We raged against the Germans but were not sure what we ought to do about them. None of us, how-ever, had any time for those who doubted the eventual outcome.

Now we were back, and with good equipment; we would show the Germans that possession of the roads was not enough in a country such as ours. We came in over the

Setesdal moors and western Telemark. I stared at the mountains and tried to get my bearings, remembering how as a boy I had shot and fished in those parts. My father owned quite a big area in these mountains.

I had also been up to the mountains beside Lake Langesæ in the summer of 1940, so as not to be in the town and have to see the Germans lording it in an occupied country. While there I caught several thousand crowns' worth of fish, which I sold for preserving, and so had something to live on the following winter. One day in September, while I was out with my nets, a stranger came down the hillside and up to the hut. It proved to be Per Jacobsen, an Oslo lad and an old companion on trips and long-distance runs. He was one of the boys who had been in the fighting at Haugsbygda in the spring. I bade him welcome to the mountains and asked how things were going in town.

'Badly,' was the answer. 'You must come down at once.'

'Why? I'm all right where I am.'

'You must come at once,' said Per. 'Sverre has come back from England, and he needs your help.'

I had been with Sverre Midtskau in the spring of 1940. At the beginning of June he had sent me a message asking if I would go with him to northern Norway. I asked for a week's grace. I had been very ill and spitting blood for several weeks; so that I had not the strength to go. Before I could get away Sverre had started.

I learned that Sverre had landed on a small island in the neighbourhood of Florö. He had been put ashore from a British submarine with an engineer and a wireless telegraphist. Their task was to set up two wireless stations, one in Trondheim and one in Oslo. Afterwards I heard the story of the landing from Sverre himself.

He told me that the submarine had surfaced in pitch darkness three and a half miles from land. They had been given a small boat to row ashore in, and after a couple of hours' rowing and baling in a choppy sea had landed on a tiny island on the outer edge of the skerries.

For a long time they had been convinced that they would go the same way as the submarine, which had dived as speedily as possible after they had been put into the boat. They slept on a heather-covered ridge on the islet, and next day rowed cautiously closer in to the shore. They landed by a small fisherman's cottage on a fair-sized island and asked the fisherman if he could take them in to Florö. The style and construction of the small boat were not at all Norwegian, and they would not be able to stand any closer investigation by German harbour police. Nor could two English wireless transmitters easily be explained away. The fisherman looked at them.

'Where have you come from in that craft?' he asked.

Sverre thought quickly, and wrongly.

'From Trondheim.'

The fisherman stared. 'Round Stadt in that little boat?' He walked round it and looked at it more closely.

'That's impossible,' he said. 'But there are so many queer people about here these days. And as long as you're not Germans I can quite well do you the service of taking you in to Florö. I can put you ashore without the Germans noticing it, too.' He smiled.

They landed at a lonely jetty in Florö.

'The boat,' said Sverre, 'you can keep that, but if anyone should ask you, you haven't seen us.'

The fisherman looked long at it.

'I think I'd better burn it,' he said. 'And for that matter, we're not great talkers hereabouts.'

I met Sverre at his parents' house, and we went into his room. He produced a box and opened it.

'I call this the "butter box", so as not to give away too much in a casual conversation,' he said.

I remember how expectantly I looked at it. It was a simple little wireless transmitter in a light-coloured wooden box.

We were greenhorns in those days where illegal work was concerned, though we fully realised that the work was not easy and that it was a game in which we were staking our lives. But it was to take many years and cost many lives to make us efficient enough to do anything against the professionals of the Gestapo.

We established ourselves in Oslo, but as we were afraid of the Germans' D/F stations we kept our own wireless station in the woods round the town. We rented a number of little huts in different places and used these as a base for operations.

The wireless set worked only on alternating current, so we had to use the lighting system. We dared not use the huts, even supposing that they had any current. We therefore connected ourselves up to the lighting system at casually chosen places in the inhabited areas and woods round about. Night after night for months on end we went out with the wireless set in a rucksack and cycled and walked for miles to find suitable places. We climbed up the electric-light poles and hooked our connections on to the wires.

Not one – not even those nearest to us – must know what was going on. In the daytime we had to do our ordinary work. We were dropping with fatigue. What kept us going was a growing pride in doing *something*, little as it was, against the hated invaders, and, paradoxically enough, the hopeless military situation of the Allies.

It was the autumn of 1940. Britain alone remained in the war against Germany. Together with small Allied groups which had escaped from their defeated countries, the island kingdom was the last defence in Europe which still held firm.

We were out night after night, carrying the wireless station about, past German road controls and barricades. We built huts of fir-boughs and dug holes in the earth, but we never got contact with England.

'Do you think they hear us?' I asked for the hundredth time.

'Don't know,' said Sverre. 'But we must clear out quickly. This is the third night from this place. And we have been trying to transmit for two hours.'

'If only we could hear something from the world outside!' I brushed the snow from my cap. 'If only we could get a few weapons sent over! Just enough to be able to defend ourselves and the wireless station if anything should happen. For that matter why didn't you bring something with you when you came?'

Sverre sighed. 'They said it was too dangerous to take them with me right through Norway from Vestlandet.'

'I don't think they've got an awful lot themselves,' I put in. 'Oh, God knows how this war will go. Our next contact may have to be made with America. We seem to be losing everywhere.'

'Are you going on for ever talking about not winning?' Sverre asked, as he prepared to move the station. 'I think we'd better go now.'

Later that autumn Sverre went back to England to establish contacts. He went by fishing-smack from Vestlandet. This traffic had now begun on a small scale: the small fishing-smacks crept out on autumn nights through the skerries, through the German patrol lines, across the North Sea to a free country. The North Sea was stormy on autumn nights, and the Germans shot anyone they caught. Thousands wanted to go over to join the Norwegian free forces, but very few had connections on the coast who could get boats for them. Sverre went about in the coastal villages making cautious inquiries.

We had arranged for a special wireless message from the B.B.C. When Sverre arrived, the Norwegian news would begin not with the usual words 'This is London with news in Norwegian,' but 'This is London with a news message in Norwegian.'

One evening it came. I rang up Per Jacobsen at once. It was dangerous to say too much on the telephone.

'The devil,' I said.

'Yes, the deuce,' said Per. 'Are you coming up?'

For safety's sake the B.B.C. continued to use the same introduction for several days. We began to regard the German troops of occupation with a certain superiority. The war was not lost yet.

Then he came back to Norway again, this time by air, sitting in a plane and peering out over the same country which we saw now. In response to a message from London, some of us had gone into the mountains, to Lake Langesæ, to receive him. Of all the special messages I received none delighted me more than that which, in December 1940, told me that Sverre was coming back.

Not knowing how the landing would take place, we waded into the fresh snow and trampled a landing-ground large enough, we thought, for a bomber. Then we carried up boughs and bushes which we had dug up from under the snow, and marked the limits of the area. 'I think we ought to get some of those chaps up here who make airfields for the Germans,' Per said.

One day an aircraft came over. We waved and signalled, but it went on. It was German.

The British plane could not find Langesæ, and the pilot wanted to turn back to England without dropping Sverre, who was coming by parachute. 'Why, your country's nothing but snow and stones and cold. It can't be much to go back to,' said a British sergeant in the aircraft.

But Sverre wanted to jump. He jumped blind and came down fifty-six miles from Langesæ. He himself landed safe and sound, but the wireless apparatus he had with him was smashed.

The next night he found us, still waiting for him in the hut at Langesæ. He had with him cigarettes and Scotch whisky, and we spent a pleasant evening in the hut. He had also brought a quantity of newspapers, including a copy of *The Times* which was two days old. We took the papers to Oslo and laid them out in the cafeteria of Oslo University, and of course this created a tremendous sensation. It was fearfully stupid, but we were still untrained in illegal work. We had not lost any of our people yet, and thought we could allow ourselves a joke.

When Sverre had been in Oslo for a little while, he was arrested, along with Max Manus. Max jumped out of a window and managed to smash himself up so badly that he was taken to Ullevaal hospital. Sverre went to Möllergata 19.[1] Luckily the Germans knew very little.

Per Jacobsen, the man who had come to Lake Langesæ to tell me that Sverre had come back to Norway, contrived to get Max out of the hospital. He contacted the doctors there and Max was moved to a single room. The German guard was chased out into the corridor – for medical reasons. The young nurse agreed to co-operate in an escape, but she insisted on being protected against reprisals. A definite night was agreed on. Late in the night she carried a rope into the room hidden under her skirt. Then she poked her chin out as far as possible and Max delivered a perfect right hook with his remaining serviceable fist. He then tried to lower himself down from the third floor by the rope but he fell down

1. *Gata* = (the) street. Möllergata 19 is normally a civil prison but during the war was used by the Germans for their political prisoners.

into the arms of Per and his helpers. After a while the German guards found the nurse unconscious, with a broken jaw.

Sverre could now lie as much as he wanted without his stories being checked with any other prisoner's account.

I was arrested myself and was kept in prison for three days. Fortunately the Germans had asked the Norwegian State Police to confine me and they let me go with an apology for having detained me.

The group which ran the Oslo wireless station was broken up, but Per would not give in. He could not rest, and started at once on illegal newspapers. He was soon arrested, however, and when, a couple of years later, the Germans were able to connect him with Sverre's trips to England, he was sent to a *Vernichtungslager*.[1] He was not the first of the boys to die, but he was the most unwearying fiery soul I met with in those first years.

The wireless station at Trondheim worked full time during the winter of 1941 and did a good job. I had managed to get work at the submarine base in Trondheim. The Germans, working at top speed, had begun turning the town into a large-scale naval base, and we had to obtain precise information about the work. My father ran a firm of surveyors and I got him, rather against his will, to take a contract with the submarine base. I was to be engineer of the concern. I had no qualifications as an engineer, but I pretended not to speak much German and kept away from the German engineers as much as I could. I was thus able to give information to the wireless station in Bymarka.[2]

Gradually, however, the game grew more and more difficult and at last I had to get one of the lads in the group appointed in my place. He really was an engineer, and he worked at the job till the following autumn.

They were smart fellows in many ways, the boys at Trondheim. They had good connections in Oslo and worked there too. One of the leaders, Björn Rörholt, proposed that we should kidnap Quisling and exhibit him in Piccadilly Circus for a crown a look. The money was to go to the

1. Lit. destruction (or liquidation) camp.
2. *Bymarka* means literally 'town land' and is the name for the country in the immediate neighbourhood of Trondheim.

27

Norwegian Fighter Fund. We had many wild plans in those days. We did get as far as obtaining a room right opposite Quisling in Erling Skjalgssons Gate in Oslo. Björn had good contacts in the telegraph service, and we were connected up with Quisling's telephone line, after which we sat and listened to all his conversations. The plan was to find out when he ordered a car so that we could pick him up in one of ours. We had ordered *hird* uniforms[1] and German police uniforms through a group in Oslo.

Once we had got Quisling into our car we would render him unconscious and drive away. On the road he would be transferred to a van and taken into the mountains. With the radio contact we had to London (S.O.E.) we hoped that an aeroplane would pick him up on a lake. Even if we had got him to London, it can be assumed that we would not have been allowed to exhibit him – inside or outside a cage.

It was the Germans who caught us – at Trondheim. They were smarter than we had given them credit for. We had been prepared for a raid on the huts in Bymarka, but instead they placed guards at the entrance to the town of Trondheim and took note of who went in and out of Bymarka at different times of the day. It was on 1st September that they struck. They caught the telegraphist on his way into the town, and by their usual methods were able to extract from him a number of names.

The telegraphist did not know my name. But I had one of the leaders of the group with me in the hut at Langesæ, where we were staying and fishing. The Gestapo came and he was caught, but I managed to escape. That was the last memory I had of Langesæ and the other well-known places beneath us.

Our pilot was unable to find the reception committee which was waiting for us down below. We cruised backwards and forwards over the Hardanger Vidda, and had to go right out to the coast to take our bearings afresh. But it was no better the second time, and we could see no light signals from the Hardanger Vidda. Once we flew over Oslo and took a bearing from there, and once I actually saw Lake Langesæ beneath us. But we could see no signals from the ground,

1. The uniforms worn by Quisling's personal guard.

so, as the pilot would not let us jump blind, we were forced to turn back. It was heart-breaking.

After escaping from the Gestapo at Langesæ I went back to Oslo, where I found I was homeless in my own town. Through some acquaintances I learned that my mother and my wife had been arrested and were being kept as hostages. My home had been ransacked by the Gestapo and the whole house turned upside down. Only my father, curiously enough, was still allowed to remain at liberty.

I telephoned Björn for news, but an obviously German voice answered:

'Björn Rörholt is not at home. From whom can I give a message?'

'No one. I want to speak to him personally.'

'Can't you come up here and wait? He'll be back soon.'

'*Heil Hitler!*' I replied, and put back the receiver.

I found Björn at last and could hardly recognise him. His fair hair was dyed coal-black. He was angry and desperate. His father and mother had been arrested and his sister put under a German guard at their home in Vettakollen. The Germans had come to Björn's home to arrest him, but, having a revolver handy, he used it and got away.

From Björn I heard more about the cleaning up at Trondheim. The organisation had been totally destroyed and the station seized. We decided we had better leave for Sweden as quickly as possible. It was arranged that a new man should take over from us and try to restart a station in Oslo.

This was my first trip across the frontier. The technical chief of the civilian A.R.P. in Oslo had long been one of our best contacts, and he promised to get us out of the town. We left Oslo in style, in one of the A.R.P.'s petrol-driven cars. This took us as far as Ski, where tickets were thrust into our hands, and we caught a train for Halden. When we reached Halden in the evening a man came to the station to meet us. We were taken to a private house and given food and coffee. Then we walked down to the Iddefjord.

At that time the Germans' system of frontier guards was not particularly good. The export organisation, on the other hand, had a first-class arrangement at the Iddefjord, whereby Norwegian refugees rowed across the fjord at night and next morning a Swedish customs official would row the boat back and moor it on the Norwegian side.

We found the boat at once. I was rather surprised to see that it was moored with iron chains instead of a rope. The noise when we cast off was alarming and would be certain, I thought, to wake the soundest sleeper among the German guards who were supposed to be a couple of hundred yards away. But we saw nothing of them, and that was what mattered.

The customs official proved to be an unusually smart fellow. The only thing we had to declare was a bottle of aquavitae, which we shared with him in return for a meal of eggs and bacon.

Early in the morning he rang up the town police at Strömstad in Sweden and told them that he had two of 'the usual kind.'

At Strömstad we were lodged in the prison for two days before being taken to Gothenburg. At Gothenburg we had a fine reception. For one reason or another we were kept at the town police station as prisoners of a sort, while waiting for a Swedish army officer to come from Stockholm to interrogate us about frontier defence works. The police in Gothenburg did all they could for us. We were not allowed to go out alone, but as long as we were accompanied by plain-clothes policemen we were allowed to visit cafés and restaurants several times a day. They bought the best things they could think of for us, just because we were Norwegians.

Finally we were interrogated by the Swedish army, and our stay in Gothenburg came to an end.

Late one dismal evening we arrived at Oereryd, where a few wretched huts were scattered about a muddy patch of ground. So this was a camp for Norwegian refugees. I had a feeling that the motto of the camp ought to be that which stood over the gate of Dante's hell: 'Abandon hope, all ye who enter here.' Hoplessness and mud were the first and overwhelming impressions, and I felt completely shattered.

Next day Björn and I discussed what we should do to get in touch with our contacts in England. In Oslo we had been in touch with the secret intelligence service. Björn also had good friends at the Legation in Stockholm, and two days later he was summoned to go there.

To be summoned to Stockholm was the greatest thing that could happen to a refugee at Oereryd. Stockholm meant the possibility of getting over to England and into the war again.

'You must inform London and see that we are sent for as quickly as possible,' I said to Björn before he started. After another two days a message came telling me to report in Stockholm.

I was not sorry to leave the camp. I had never come to understand the tragedy of the refugee as I did in the short time I was there. There he is, without money or friends, with the blackest despair in his heart, and he is put in a place where the only thing that matters is to keep him alive. The refugee is homeless in his own country. Wherever he goes, he will in the best event be tolerated.

When I got to Stockholm I was summoned to the military attaché's office. Björn had done good work: our friends in the secret intelligence service wanted both Björn and myself to go to England as soon as possible, but first there was more work to be done in Norway.

I was to go back to Oslo and get the work started. I was also to see if it was possible to do anything about getting Sverre and the boys from Trondheim out of prison.

At the police station I was provided with money and various papers which might be of use to me. In those days the great illegal military apparatus in Stockholm had not been established, and the secret conferences which I had with the chiefs took place in the lavatory. There we would sit and talk for several hours.

The Swedish frontier control was considered more difficult to get through than the German, but the Norwegian military men in Stockholm already had some experience. Late one autumn evening I got off a train in the depths of the Swedish province of Värmland. So as not to arouse suspicion I was dressed in ordinary clothes with a peaked cap, and carried a suitcase. I looked like a Swedish farm hand who had been on a trip into town to pick up girls.

I presented a chit to a Swedish station-master and said 'sykkel' (bicycle) with the best Swedish accent I could muster. The bicycle had been sent from Stockholm a few days before. So the work began. In reality it was neither particularly dangerous nor difficult to cross the frontier between Sweden and Norway; it was only a question of prolonged toil and trouble.

I was to cycle for fifty or sixty miles through Värmland. I was then to leave the bicycle near Finnskogen, and walk thirty-five miles to an address I had been given on the Norwegian side.

I had always considered myself pretty good at finding my way, but the Legation, which lacked everything in those days, had no proper maps of the frontier districts. All I had was a Swedish motoring map on which the scale was $1:500,000$. It was not surprising that I made one mistake after another. At last I was so worn out that I hardly knew which was north on the compass, but on the third day I reached my destination in Norway – Vestby, a small farm two or three miles from the frontier. My clothes and suitcase were ruined. As I looked then I certainly could not have deceived anyone by pretending to be a peaceful Swede.

I went into the farmer's house at Vestby. It was the first time I was to be received as an honoured guest just because I had come from abroad. The farmer produced the best food he had. When I had eaten I fell asleep at the table; the journey had worn me out. I was put to bed and slept for a whole twenty-four hours.

There was a young girl living in the house at Vestby, who pressed my clothes and put all my things in order while I was asleep. Time after time I had fallen into bog-holes and obviously could not go to Oslo looking as I did. I was well provided with money and wanted to pay her for the work. But she gave me an answer which I have remembered ever since: 'I don't want money. This is the only thing I can do, and I want to do something.'

I took the up train and arrived in Oslo the same evening. I went immediately to see one of the boys. He himself was not at home, but his mother had gradually become accustomed to living in an occupied country, and she took me in without asking any questions.

The boys were full of enthusiasm when we met. They thought the illegal work could now go ahead in earnest.

Every little report or scrap of information gave them encouragement and fresh hope.

The carrying out of my tasks was not a hundred per cent successful. I got in touch with a number of men who were carrying on illegal work in Oslo, and we planned the setting up of a station which could send messages to London through the sea by means of ultra-short waves. One of the boys had contact with the Michelsen institute in Bergen, and the people there were to deliver the whole apparatus. Another plan was to connect up an automatic transmitter with the German navy's own telegraph line between Oslo and Bergen. All messages over this line would then be sent direct to London.

We laid many plans for getting Sverre and the boys from Trondheim out of prison. I resumed our earlier contact with the telegraph administration, and we sat for a long time in an office in the centre of Oslo listening to Victoria Terrace.[1] The plan was to find out how orders were given between Victoria Terrace and Möllergata 19. Then we ourselves could one day order the boys to be moved from No. 19 to Victoria Terrace, and hold up the car on the way. We were short of everything – men, arms and, indeed, the courage to execute the coup. In short, we were not yet ready to fight the Gestapo with its own weapons.

When I had been in Oslo a few weeks, I realised that it would take a long time to get our friends out of prison. There was nothing to be done but to return to Sweden and hand over the work to others. All the same, I had obtained valuable information to take with me to England.

I recrossed the frontier by the way I had come. The boys in Oslo had got me a better map, and I had no difficulty in finding the bicycle which was hidden near Finnskogen, about thirty-five miles from the frontier, on the Swedish side. But it was now November, and the snow had come. I had to wade along through a foot of snow. Even on the roads there was a great deal of snow, as the Swedes did not trouble to clear them. Late one afternoon I arrived at Sunne. Although I was in good fettle, I had been struggling along for two days and had spent the night out in the snow,

1. The headquarters of the Gestapo in Norway.

so I was pretty weary.

Then I did a thing which one ought never to do when carrying out illegal work. I was tired and I needed food and rest, and I was audacious enough to go into a hotel. Seeing my battered condition, the head waiter eyed me sceptically. But he became politeness itself when I asked for the most expensive things. I ate and drank, bought the best liqueur in the hotel, and as it was getting late, I got the head waiter to buy a ticket for me and send off the bicycle by train. As usual, the Swedish police had men posted at the booking-offices in the frontier towns to listen for Norwegian speech. This time they were tricked.

When I arrived in Stockholm I submitted a report. I spent a few cheerful days in the Capital of the North before receiving orders to report at the airfield where I was to take off for England. Life in Stockholm was hectic; spies from every part of Europe were assembled there. We who were carrying on illegal work for Norway occasionally allowed ourselves the relaxation of a visit to the best Stockholm restaurants.

Then England – a long year of schooling and waiting to return to Norway.

Now we were again over Norway; but the pilot could not find his way to the place he was making for and would not let us jump. Was he really going to take us back to England again? Yes, he really was. We were flying westwards and nearing the coast.

Suddenly the aircraft made one or two sharp turns. The German anti-aircraft had detected us and were firing at the plane. Not feeling particularly cheerful, we sat on our thin sheet of aluminium and heard the projectiles whizzing by in the dark. When we peered out, we could see little sparks far below; they moved slowly up, became large and menacing, and passed with a roar. The pilot turned and twisted as he worked his way out over the sea. Gradually all grew quiet around us. The North Sea was beneath us again.

I thought of Sverre, whom we were hoping to free from Möllergata 19. Later I learned that he had escaped without our help. One of the cleaners had been able to steal the key of a strategically placed door on the third floor. The door opened on to the staircase leading into the southern tower, and this in turn gave access to the outside world. No one knew how the cleaner had got hold of the key – but he had it, and he was willing to help Sverre and his cell companions to get out. The Germans had discovered that Sverre had been in England, and it was certain that he would be sentenced to death. One day the cleaner unlocked the door of the cell; Sverre and his two comrades went quietly along the corridor and let themselves out through the door. They managed to make their way to the Stortorv,[1] where they got on a tram and disappeared. This gave the Germans something to think about. Several times they turned the whole prison upside down; even the wood-piles in the yard were unstacked.

We landed in Scotland with one engine severely damaged and one on fire. The Germans had succeeded in hitting us.

We were still in a bad temper because we had not been allowed to jump out when we were over Norway. Moreover, we were cold and frozen stiff, and could hardly move when the plane stopped after landing. Even 'the Chicken', who came from the forests and cold winters of the Oesterdal, was as stiff as a statue when he crawled out.

His real name was Hans Storhaug, and he was a sergeant. For some reason he had once been called 'the Chicken' and thereafter was known by no other name. I myself had acquired a fine nickname; I was called 'the General'. The pilot must have heard the boys using this name. When we abused him roundly because he had not let us jump blind, he looked at me and, thinking no doubt of the cold, windswept Hardanger Vidda, said :

'I thought it looked *too* bad to drop a general.'

1. A large central square in Oslo.

2. ENGLAND

We were put in a hut close to the airfield, and the British security officers took care that no one came near us. Our first trip having failed, no one must know where we had been or where we were going. For the first few hours we just lay and slept. We were tired and worn out by waiting, and cold and stiff after sitting, ready to jump, behind the open hole in the aircraft. We were angry, too. We had been ready to leave a whole month earlier, but the weather had been so bad that no attempt was made. Now we should have to wait for another new moon and a new opportunity.

It was agreed that we would ask to be sent to some out-of-the-way place to continue our training. We did not want to return to the Section and the curiosity of our friends – nor did we want to hang about in London. We knew the life of the great city well enough already, from leaves and other expeditions. . . .

I remembered how I was received when I came from Sweden to London for the first time. Two British officers were waiting at the railway station and I was given a splendid welcome.

For security reasons I was not taken to the ordinary training camp where refugees were screened and interrogated. Instead, the officers asked if I would like to see a bit of life, and we went straight to a night club. It was made clear that the War Office would be paying the bill, and both the young men had an interest in making the fullest use of this opportunity. It was a lively evening and night, and my first glimpse of the variegated life of London during the war. Uniforms of all the Allied nations were to be seen at the places of entertainment. What struck a foreigner was that practically all the women were in uniform. The only ones who were not seemed to be the tarts in Piccadilly Circus, and these too were engaged in war service in their own way.

London had been sorely wounded by the German attacks the year before. Ruined houses and bombed blocks of flats made gaps in the vista of the streets. One area in the heart of the City was just a desert of ruins: only the streets remained, running empty and purposeless between heaps of fallen masonry. But, amid all this devastation, the untidy city and the pale men and women living in it possessed strength and dignity enough to give new hope and courage to us who had lost our fatherland.

For one coming from an occupied country and from neutral Sweden, it was marvellous to see active military operations. Here there were barrage balloons, and fighters always in the air. Spiritual weapons can be very effective, but for raising and encouraging morale physical ones are invaluable. There is nothing more depressing for an active nature than to stand before an enemy unarmed. The feeling of hopeless material inferiority leads to the abandonment of belief in one's self, and only the strongest can resist it. Even under the hottest rain of bombs one could see how the English took courage afresh when they spoke of the Spitfire as the best fighter in the world.

I met in London the head of the Norwegian section of the secret intelligence service. After I had submitted a report to him, he proposed that I should try to return to Norway on a secret mission. I said I thought the liberation of Norway must be effected by force of arms. During the fighting in Norway I had felt the lack of proper military training, and now asked if I could have some instruction in the use of weapons. Yes, there was a section which was just the thing for me. I was sent to the Linge Company with a recommendation. This was my first meeting with Captain Linge. He made a very strong impression by his winning nature. This was at the beginning of December, 1941. Three weeks later he was killed in action at Maaloy.

I went first to Special Training School No. 3 near Southampton. Here I found nearly thirty Norwegian boys from all parts of the country and of all classes of society. It was evident that they had tried to get men with the greatest possible variety of experience. We began our first exercises in the use of small arms and explosives.

Apart from our activities, it was very peaceful in the

south of England. The only sign of the war was that the village inns were full of soldiers in the evenings.

The Germans called the school for secret sabotage troops in England a 'gangster school', and from a purely practical standpoint they were undoubtedly right. We not only learnt to force locks and break open safes, but we were taught the use of explosives in all circumstances, both in battle and elsewhere. It is incredible what a man can do with a handful of explosive placed at the right place at the right time – he can halt an army or devastate the machinery on which a whole community depends. We learned to use pistols, knives and poison, together with the weapons nature had given us – our fists and feet. 'Never give a man a chance' were words we were always hearing. 'If you've got him down, kick him to death.'

'This is your only friend,' the instructor reminded us, holding up a pistol, 'the only friend you can rely on. Treat him properly and he'll take care of you.' But in spite of all this we were not gangsters.

There is no other law in war than this: that one has got to win. By German military standards, no doubt, our methods were unworthy of a soldier. The Germans had tried to create a tradition of warfare, and had painted a pretty, but touched-up picture of the chivalrous German warrior. Perhaps they did not realise how false the picture was. No warfare is chivalrous, and least of all their own.

We, who came from a small oppressed country, gladly resorted to every method which could injure the enemy. For the underdog cannot afford to carry on war according to the rules of the stronger party. When we had learnt our tricks from the preparatory courses in the Linge Company, we were ready to return to Norway and put them to the test.

But we had not yet reached this stage, and when the school in the south of England closed down, we were sent to another in Scotland. Here we soon learnt that we had become part of a vast organisation which carried on sabotage and espionage all over Europe, and which was divided into different sections for the different countries concerned. After a time in the extreme north of Scotland, we were sent south to a place in the neighbourhood of Inverness, and here we first entered the training school of the Norwegian section. This was near Aviemore, among some of the wildest mountains in Scotland.

The soldiers in the camp made a strange collection; all had fled from Norway and come to England for a chance to continue the fight against the Germans. Everybody had just one thing in his head – to get home and start afresh.

We lived a good, tiring, open-air life. There were quantities of roe deer and stags in the mountains, and the rivers were full of salmon. Because of the war there were few who had leisure to profit legitimately from these good things, and the Scottish authorities were ready to turn a blind eye to our expeditions to get meat and fish for the camp. The British soldiers' rations were comparatively slender for the big Norwegian lads, and without extras from the mountains and rivers we should have lived much less well than we did. We ourselves, however, set a limit on our shooting; not more than five stags might be shot in one week. One of the boys was unfortunate; he was caught deer-stalking by a land-owner and had to fork out a five pounds' fine for poaching.

The object of the life was clear. We were to learn to fend for ourselves, like the men of ancient Sparta.

We got on well with the Scottish people. I do not know where the stories of Scottish parsimony originate, but they cannot possibly refer to the Scotsmen with whom we came in contact. We could buy eggs, milk and all farm produce whenever we liked, and at reasonable prices. We drank and celebrated with the Scotsmen, and they understood our peculiarities. They used to say, 'I'm sure you'll soon be back in your own country,' and this was the best thing they could wish us.

The boys came and went. Suddenly we would find that some of them were missing, but no one asked where they had gone. They returned, and no one asked where they had come from. We grew smarter and smarter every day. Only one care oppressed us continually and gnawed at all our hearts: we knew that the people at home were having a bad time, and that they were just sitting and waiting for the day when we should return. We who were to return to Norway could read Norwegian papers, and we received regular reports from the supreme command of our own armed forces so that we might follow what was happening at home.

We were sent on a parachute course at Special Training School (S.T.S.) 51, in the neighbourhood of Manchester. I think most of us were afraid when we jumped for the first time. But if we were to go home, we must learn to use our parachutes, so we consoled ourselves with the old proverb: 'If the first umbrella doesn't open, we can just put up another.'

While at S.T.S.3 we had practised jumping from a high platform. One day the Commandant wanted to have a try. He broke both his legs.

Then one day I found myself sitting in a small basket hanging beneath a barrage balloon. The balloon rose higher and higher, and I confess that I was alarmed. When it began to swing to and fro, the ground beneath us swung as well. I looked upwards so as not to feel giddy, but the sky and clouds were swinging too.

The instructor was the first man to jump. I was to be number two, and was sitting ready on the edge of the basket. I saw the cars nearly a thousand feet below, no bigger than lozenges. I had told the man in charge of the balloon to give the orders quickly, and he did: 'Action station' and 'go' came in the same breath.

It is unpleasant to jump out into space with something like a heavy rucksack fastened to one's back, but a grand feeling when the parachute has opened. Later on we jumped from aircraft, and then we jumped in the dark.

When it blew hard we were not allowed to jump, but one day when the wind force was greater than the normal maximum, the officer in charge said, 'Send up the Norwegians; they always manage all right.' The important thing was to free oneself from the parachute as quickly as possible after reaching the ground. The man who jumped after me landed in a potato field, and was unable to free himself from the parachute at once. He was dragged for a long way with potatoes flying up behind him as if he were a mechanical potato-digger. A few men were standing by a ditch looking on. We went up to them and said:

'You ought to try this; it's good fun.'

'No!' They shook their heads long and seriously. 'Not after seeing that.'

Four of our comrades had got so far that they had been dropped over Norway to establish a base for operations. There they were, waiting for more of us to follow them. They were now waiting for the next moon, when there would be chance of our being able to join them on the Hardanger Vidda. It was hard enough for us to wait, but those fellows were out on the Vidda, alone in the winter cold. They had been there for many months.

The leader of the group was Jens Anton Paulsson, tall, gaunt, and a good hillman. We had poached many a stag together, and I knew he was in his element where shooting and fishing were concerned. He was, moreover, a sober fellow with sound judgment. He would manage all right where he was, for the Vidda was his own home country.

Arne Kjelstrup was a plumber from Oslo and second in command. His inexhaustible humour might be coming in useful just then. He could be pugnacious too: after the campaign in Norway was over, he and another man collected a quantity of arms and ammunition and attacked a whole German column at Kringen. The two of them fired till their weapons grew hot, and then cleared off. Arne still had a German bullet in his hip, acquired during the fighting in the Stryken valley. Fortunately the bullet had first hit a large wire-cutter which he had about him, and this had saved him from greater injury.

Knut Haugland was tall and thin, like Jens, and was the party's wireless operator. Claus Helberg, another member, was the sort of man who might at any moment have a piece of bad luck and get into fearful difficulties, but he had also a remarkable capacity for getting out of them.

This party was called Grouse (*Rype* in Norwegian). Because of their knowledge of the locality, they were assigned to a special group in the school which was earmarked to return and operate in the province of Telemark.

One lone pioneer had gone over even before Grouse. This was Einar Skinnarland, a young engineer from the Hydro works in Rjukan. Einar had wanted to go to England to join the Norwegian forces. He went over by the simple way of taking a coastal steamer from Egersünd in Norway to Aberdeen in Scotland – in war time.

One of the Company Linge men, Lt. Strarheim, had been in

Norway on a job and wanted to go back to England. He collected a group of adventurous young men around him and boarded the coastal steamer in Egersünd late one evening in March, 1942. They bought tickets to Stavanger like any other peaceful traders. Well out from the harbour they hijacked the ship with crew, cargo and passengers. The captain was ordered to set a course for Aberdeen. They had a radio set with them and informed S.O.E. The R.A.F. gave them fighter cover from dawn until they entered British waters.

Professor Tronstad and S.O.E. immediately saw the advantages of a man like Einar Skinnarland. If they could get him quickly back to Rjukan, they would have an established resident who could furnish them with information. The problem was to get Einar back to his home and his work before he was missed. The Gestapo had already established their labour control. Einar was still on his Easter vacation. There was no time to give him a parachute training course, so after a day crammed with instructions he was flown over Norway and parachuted down on the Hardanger Vidda. He skied back home and reported for work.

His line of communication to England was to be via Sweden on an illegal postal route to a cover address in Stockholm.

But for an unfortunate accident, I should have gone with the four men of the Telemark group who were already established on the Hardanger Vidda. We had been ready to start in the spring of 1942, but the plan was put off till the autumn on account of the light nights. During a field exercise I stumbled with a loaded pistol in my hand, and put a bullet through the sole of my foot. I was recovering in hospital when the Grouse party was formed, and soon I heard that they had been flown over and landed at Fjarefit in the Songedal. Thence its members were to make their way to the Mösvass dam area, and were to receive a detachment of British commando troops who were to land by glider on the great Skoland marshes.

In the continuous bad weather which prevailed on the Vidda, it took the boys a month to reach the Skoland marshes with the heavy equipment. As soon as they had arrived London notified them that the gliders were coming.

The allies had long been aware of the importance of heavy

water.[1] By using uranium fission, one could construct an atomic pile and produce a nearly unlimited amount of energy. Besides energy, such a pile would produce a number of radioactive elements. One of these was an artificial element (the heaviest ever discovered) which was called plutonium. Plutonium was, beside the uranium isotope 235, the second great atomic explosive.

To make an atomic pile produce, however, one needed a substance which would 'slow down' the neutrons from the uranium without absorbing them. In this way one could get a controlled chain reaction. This substance, called a moderator, would have to surround the uranium and several tons would be necessary. On both sides of the front line scientists at that time came to the conclusion that very pure graphite or heavy water were the only two substances suitable. Even minute impurities in the graphite would prevent the production of energy, and consequently the production of plutonium. The factory at Vemork in Rjukan was the only plant in Europe with a production of heavy water on a commercial scale – about two tons a year. The allied governments and war offices, who knew how far they themselves had advanced towards an atomic bomb, were deadly scared. The production of heavy water at Rjukan had to be stopped.

In the autumn of 1941 the War Office considered three methods for an attack on Vemork; bombing, sabotage or airborne troops.

Bombing was considered impracticable, partly because of the difficulties of finding the works but also because large quantities of liquid ammonia were stored there. If they were hit and destroyed, the town would have been wiped out in a

1. As the name indicates, heavy water is heavier than ordinary water – about 11%. It is found in all water in a ratio of 1 to 5,000. The atoms of hydrogen in heavy water have been replaced by atoms with a nucleus of one proton and one neutron, instead of just one proton as in ordinary water. Its chemical sign is D_2O.

At Vemork it was obtained as a by-product under the electrolysis of water to produce ordinary hydrogen for the manufacture of ammonia. This electrolylic process requires very large amounts of electric power – direct current. The Vemork factory was, before and during the war, the world's greatest producer of this D_2O. Before the war the output was only about 10 kilograms per month. During the war it came up to about 200 kilograms at its peak.

few minutes. The use of saboteurs was rejected, although it later proved successful. It was decided to use airborne troops from British Airborne Division and a group from an engineering unit was selected. These troops would be transported by gliders to the Skoland marshes about fifteen miles west of Rjukan. From there our four Norwegians from Grouse would guide them into Rjukan and Vemork. They would blow up the heavy water plant, and if possible also the direct current electrical plant.

Forty-five men and N.C.O.s, led by a lieutenant, were chosen for the job. After its completion they were to split up in small groups and try to reach Sweden; including the four airmen from the two gliders. This task I regarded as impossible. With lack of skis and ski-ing capability they would have to keep to the few roads and pass through all inhabited areas, and would be caught by the Germans.

It never went this far.

On the night of 19th-20th November, two Halifax aircraft, each with a glider Horsas Mk.1, started from Skiffen airfield near Wick in Scotland. They met with bad weather and icing conditions. The Norwegian group Grouse was supplied with a Eureka homing radiobeam, but to no avail. The aircraft did not find them.

The aircraft with their gliders tried to return home. One aircraft and its glider crashed on its way to Norway, south of Stavanger. The crew of the aircraft were all killed outright. Three men in the glider were killed – they have never been identified – and the remaining sixteen were offered all assistance to escape by the local Norwegian population. But the oldest commanding officer refused to imperil the civilians and surrendered to the Germans. They were sent to Egersünd and, according to the civilian population, tortured before they were shot. They were buried in unmarked graves with the men from the aircraft, on the beach near Ogna, north of Egersünd. Their graves were marked and tended by the Norwegians until the end of the war when all were dug up and buried with military honours in Egenes graveyard in Stavanger.

The other aircraft lost its glider due to icing of the tow rope and crashed into the mountainside north of Stavanger. The two airmen, the Commanding Officer and seven men were killed outright and four were badly wounded. The rest were taken prisoner by the Germans. The four wounded were taken to a German hospital and killed. Their bodies were weighted down with heavy stones and sunk in the sea. They were never found. Five men survived the crash unwounded. They were taken prisoner and were later placed in the big concentration camp at Grini, near Oslo, where they were kept in isolation. On 18th January, 1943 they were taken to Trandum and shot. Their bodies have been found in a big mass grave with one hundred and fifty-seven Norwegians and forty-six Russians.

No one knows by what means the Germans got the story of the operation.

After this disaster, the whole defence of Rjukan was strengthened and a minefield was laid around the factory. The Germans then felt assured that their precious plant should be safe from another attack.

At the same time in England, a new group was formed to go to Norway, and was given the code name 'Gunnerside'. I had just come out of hospital when Professor Leif Tronstad told me one day that I was to go with it. Professor Tronstad, an expert on Norwegian industry, was a member of Section IV of the Supreme Command of the Armed Forces, and told us all that was known of the unsuccessful operation. The shooting of the men taken prisoner from the gliders was a serious war crime, he told us. It would be taken up at the end of the war. Meanwhile it was not usual, he continued, for soldiers to be given information about operations other than those with which they themselves were connected, but he and Colonel Wilson, who was in charge of sabotage work in Scandinavia, had thought it best to explain the whole situation to us. We must be prepared to receive no better treatment than the British soldiers if we were taken prisoner. The intention now was that we should start as soon as possible. The matter was the more urgent because the Grouse party was waiting for us. Tronstad had received a report that they were short of boots, clothes, food, arms and ammunition. So the Gunnerside group was made ready for action as quickly as possible.

With the help of photographs and drawings we planned the action with Tronstad in the most minute detail. We were to land in the mountains, and after getting in touch with

Grouse we were to go down the hillside on the north side of the valley near Vaaer. We were then to cross the Maan river somewhere halfway between Rjukan and Vemork and follow the railway line to the factory, where, according to reports from Grouse, there were fifteen men on guard. The work done, we were to return by the same route. If anyone was cut off or wounded, it would be possible, Tronstad said, to hide either in the factory, behind a tool-shed outside the gate, or in a cable intake under the floor.

After the operation the Grouse and Gunnerside groups were to withdraw to Sweden; but Arne, Einar, Knut Haugland and I were to remain in the mountains to establish a permanent base and organise home forces in the district.

The British had taken a number of air photographs of Rjukan and the area round the factory. Tronstad had been technical adviser when the works were being planned, and knew the factory inside out. But sometimes we raised some special question which he could not answer, and then he took it away and gave us the answer next day. So we guessed that he was in contact with someone who knew the factory even better than he did.

One day when I was up in Tronstad's office he took out a large brief-case and showed it to me. Like most of the papers at the Supreme Command of the Armed Forces it was marked 'strictly secret'. But this brief-case had an additional inscription : 'Unofficial for Supreme Command of Armed Forces.'

'It's the heavy water,' said Tronstad. 'It's manufactured at Vemork, and can be used for some of the dirtiest work that can possibly be imagined. If the Germans can solve the problem, they'll win the war.' Tronstad turned over some papers in the brief-case, and I could see that it had to do with splitting the atom.

One day Colonel Wilson and Tronstad wished to have a talk with me alone.

'We know that according to the plan you and Arne, with Einar, are to remain behind on the Hardanger Vidda to establish a base there,' said Wilson, 'but Tronstad and I would rather that you all went to Sweden. The Germans will be fearfully upset if you succeed in blowing up Vemork.'

Tronstad put in, 'They will do all they can to catch you. We can't run such a risk as to have our men operating on the

Hardanger Vidda.'

I became quite desperate. I stuttered and stammered, and produced all the best arguments I could. 'They won't find us. We are accustomed to the mountains – in country we know. We can live on the mountains and the wilderness. I won't go back to England. I shall never come back again however long the war may last.' I grew quite excited. 'Those louts won't catch us.'

Wilson and Tronstad gave way at last. But they had given me something to think about.

After a short course in industrial sabotage at Special Training School No. 17 we were ready for the task at Vemork. We had seen models of heavy-water apparatus and had practice in preparing the charges which were to be used. The training was carried out under conditions resembling as closely as possible those which we were expecting to meet.

On the last day at No. 17, after we had gone over the final plans, Tronstad made a little speech to us.

'You must reckon that the Germans will in no circumstances take any prisoners. For the sake of those who have gone before, and who are now dead, I ask you to do your best to make the operation a success. You all know how important it is, but what you are doing now will live in Norway's history in a hundred years' time.'

With Tronstad's words in our minds we were sent to Special Training School No. 61, an establishment in a country house in the neighbourhood of Cambridge. It was a station for people who were going to Europe on secret errands, and who had to wait for planes. The place was very closely guarded. A number of service women kept the house in order, cooked the meals and gave the men some social life. They belonged to the special section called 'Fannies'. These girls did an uncommonly good job, seeing that everything went as it should and doing their best to prevent the delays from getting on our nerves. And, when the Commandant suggested it, they were always willing to come to Cambridge in the evening for a little party. The Commandant would organise a party if he were reasonably sure there would not be an operation next day. But if we asked the Fannies about our comrades who had gone out before us, they became dumb and knew nothing.

The Fannies had their own cars, and very fine ones. When

we drove into Cambridge of an evening it was usually to the best restaurant in the city where we would eat and drink at the expense of the War Office; the main thing being to enjoy ourselves as much as possible before we went the way of the gliders.

Modern war has swept away all our former ideas of time and distance. We might be drinking champagne in Cambridge one evening and landing in the snow on the cold and lonely Hardanger Vidda the next. Joachim Rönneberg was a conscientious chief, and saw that we were home early, got plenty of sleep, and were always ready for an operation at any given moment. The Chicken and I frequently prophesied that the next day would be like the day before, with more waiting, more wearisome mental contrasts between the green English winter landscape – green grass and ceaseless rain – and the conditions of the Hardanger Vidda where the Grouse party were waiting – snow, wind, and wild storm-swept expanses.

'Let's go home now,' Rönneberg would say. The Chicken and I grumbled, while the girls agreed with us that there was both time and necessity for another bottle. But it usually ended in Rönneberg getting his way. We would then go out to look for Kasper Idland, who used to go on expeditions of his own, and get him to come home too. The girls took good care of us in other ways too. They saw that we did not talk to strangers, that we did not catch cold, and that we came home in good order. We had a feeling of being fenced in and protected at every point from the dangers and difficulties of this world – that we might be used for one single purpose at home in Norway.

All the same we kicked over the traces now and then. The country round the estate was full of beautiful pheasants, which made excellent eating. Occasionally we would crawl out through the barbed wire fence, and shoot the birds with pistols in the fields and copses. Special Training School No. 61 was a fearfully secret place. Sometimes the neighbouring farmers complained to the Commandant that strange bandits were shooting on their land, but the Commandant was not aware that he had any visitors at the house at all. That people who did not exist could shoot pheasants was, he said, impossible. The Chicken swore that this was better sport than all the capercailzie-shooting in the Oesterdal, and both the Fannies and we agreed that we could have no better food than roast pheasant.

It is a curious thing about English cooking that the best food is often cooked in the dirtiest kitchen. When one of the boys took a fancy to one of the prettiest Fannies, he would spend whole days scrubbing a kitchen table – and it needed it. We often washed and scrubbed for hours just to kill time. But however long we kept at it the Fannies were always just as amiable – and unapproachable.

The three months we spent at S.T.S. No. 61 were a severe trial to our nerves. All the time we were waiting for the weather over Norway to improve enough for us to fly over the Hardanger Vidda and jump. But in the winter of 1942-3 there was continual bad weather. The bombers could only just get over Norway at night, and if they were to have any chance of finding what they were looking for there must be moonlight. The desperate part of it was that the Grouse party was out there waiting for us, with little food and poor equipment. Many of us would have been in a worse state of nerves, however, if the British had not sent us to so homely and pleasant a place.

At last, one day in January 1943, we stood on the airfield, full of expectation. Tronstad himself had come to wish us good luck.

As a last good-bye to England we had our death pills served out to us on the airfield. The pill was a little rubber capsule containing zyankalium. One could hold it in one's mouth, and if one was unlucky enough to swallow it whole it would, it was said, go right through one and come out without doing any harm. No one felt any desire to test it. If one bit it to pieces death was guaranteed in five seconds.

A spy in civilian clothes usually has it sewn into his lapel so as to be able to get it into his mouth without too much difficulty. We were in battledress with camouflage suits on top. It was a struggle to squeeze the pill down into the pocket for the field service bandage, which is on one's thigh. The boys cursed. 'If we're to get hold of it without using our hands, we must be born acrobats.'

It was a terrible disappointment when we had to turn back after a four hours' search for Grouse. We had been over the Hardanger Vidda. We had seen Lake Langesæ, seen

Norwegian people outside their houses, even Norwegian dogs on the roads. And then, cold and stiff, we were standing on an English airfield again.

At our own request we were moved to a solitary place, where we waited for the next full moon. A little stone house with white window-frames on an island in the north of Scotland was placed at our disposal. We went for long walks on the moors and in the hills, shot seal and stags. It was lonely, healthy and tedious. The winter was even wetter than it is in Vestlandet.

There were many old Norwegian names in the district. But everywhere we came upon abandoned farms, where wood and wild were steadily encroaching on the fields.

Could the weather in Norway be as bad as it was there? When the full moon was nearly due in February, we were sent back to the south again. But the weather there was no better. We had not much more than a week in hand, and the first days had already gone. At eleven each morning a notice was put up saying whether an operation for our section might be expected in the evening. 'No operation to-day,' was the continual refrain. Sometimes we were told to be ready to start that evening. But in the course of the day a polite supervisor would come and tell us that the order had been cancelled. The full moon came, and there were only a few days left. One day we waited a long time for the supervisor. He did not come. Were we at last to attempt a new landing on the Hardanger Vidda and meet the Grouse lads again? In the evening we went in cars to the airfield.

3. WE MEET GROUSE

At the airfield it was raining in torrents. The place was only used for secret undertakings, and the personnel there had seen the setting-out of many queer expeditions. Nevertheless they stared when a party of heavily armed soldiers in white camouflage suits, and with parachutes on their backs, came trudging through the rain. Once more Professor Tronstad was on the spot and wished us good luck.

It was a tight fit inside the aircraft. With our heavy equipment, weapons and thick clothes, we could hardly move at all. We flung ourselves down and the door was slammed to. From the rainy weather in England we crossed to a cold, clear moonlight night over Norway.

Again we came in over the Hardanger Vidda.

A message came from the pilot that we were to jump in another ten minutes. This time we were not to search for the reception committee. The hole in the bottom of the plane was opened, and all preparations made. Parachute jumping always involves a certain strain, whether one has done it before or not, and no doubt the hearts of most of us beat a little faster at the thought that we were about to jump out into the moonlight over heaven knew what. The warning lamp in the roof burned green: all clear! The first man – Joachim – went through the hole with a tremendous clatter and disappeared. Then, in quick succession, another man – two packages – three more men – two packages. I prepared to jump. The English assistant pressed himself close to the side of the plane, but on the wrong side. The line fastening my parachute to the plane was wound round his body in such a way that I should carry him with me when I jumped. Catching hold of him, I pushed him over to the other side, and jumped from a standing position; there was not time to sit down.

At the moment of jumping the aircraft is flying at a speed of sixty yards per second. Seconds are valuable. If one hesitates for ten seconds, one will find oneself six hundred yards away from one's comrades.

The string which attached my parachute to the aircraft, and which would open it, had broken like a severed umbilical cord. The distance to the ground was 650 feet and the distance back was hundreds and hundreds of miles. Then I felt the marvellous jerk which told me that the parachute had opened.

While I hung in the air I saw the plane disappearing northwards, returning to England – to rain, to nice hot tea, to a party to-morrow. Beneath me there was nothing but snow and ice. Here lay the Hardanger Vidda, the largest, loneliest and wildest mountain area in northern Europe. Some four thousand square miles of naked mountains, at a height of about four thousand feet above sea level. Only for a short time in summer does a little grass and moss grow up among the rocks and snow. No human beings live on these desolate expanses, only the creatures of the wilds; here are large herds of reindeer, which shun mankind and whose wants are small.

I landed with all the containers round me. Through a misunderstanding the pilot had dropped the containers last instead of first. I set to work to shut up the parachute, so that our equipment might not be carried away. One of the parcels containing rucksacks set off at a high speed towards the end of a long lake. Birger Stromsheim ran after it and caught hold of it, but he too sailed right away till both man and material were held fast in a crack in the ice.

It was marvellous to be able to sit down in the snow, lay one's hand on it and look round. We were in Norway again – six free Norwegian soldiers up on the Hardanger Vidda. The Chicken was delighted to put on skis. The Westcountrymen – Fredrik Kayser, Joachim, Birger and Kasper – would have their work cut out if they tried to keep up with him. Many had given up trying to follow him over a long distance.

The ground was quite strange to us – long, low, snow-clad hills, typical of the central or eastern parts of the Hardanger Vidda.

'Do you know where we are?' asked Joachim.

'We may be in China for all I know,' I had to confess. 'I don't know this place.'

But morning was not far off, and everything had to be cleared up and stowed away before daylight.

One of the men made a reconnaissance and came back with a splendid piece of news: there was a hut close by. We toiled and moiled and managed to get everything under the snow just before daybreak. Tired but happy we went over to the hut, loosened the frame of the door with an axe and went in. It was a fine, large hut. The best thing of all was that there was half a fathom of birch wood in it.

The great question was where we could be. Could this be the Bjornesfjord, where, according to the plan, we were to have been dropped? I could not think that anyone would cart wood so far into the mountains. But before we could find out where we were we must rest and have a good sleep.

We tumbled into bed in the hut-owner's best bedclothes.

During the afternoon all preparations for our departure were made. We did not know for certain where we were, but reckoned that we must be in the neighbourhood of the Bjornesfjord. A course was laid which would correspond to the route from the Bjornesfjord to Lake Saure, where we were to meet Grouse.

We buried in the snow all the things we did not require immediately, carefully marking the places. As soon as it started to grow dark we set off. We had not gone many miles before the wind began to rise, and it was clear that a storm was coming on. Night was approaching; we were in country we did not know and on a route of which we were not sure. With the weather looking as it did, we thought it most prudent to return to the hut and await developments.

That night there broke one of the worst storms I have ever experienced in the mountains. We could be thankful that we were under cover. The gale raged for three days with such violence that we could not go out of doors, and we all in turn became more or less unwell. The sudden change of climate from sea level and green fields in England to hard midwinter four thousand feet up on the Hardanger Vidda gave us a sort of climate sickness. The symptoms were a temperature and a severe inflammation of the glands in the neck.

When the third day came, and the gale began to abate, we all felt slack and in poor condition for travel. The storm had so changed the face of the ground that we only found our stores of provisions with difficulty. We realised that it was dangerous to bury things in the snow, even the whole cargo of an aircraft. For what had been a valley the evening before had now become a height. We spent the whole morning searching for our things, and then began to make fresh preparations for departure. We now knew where we were and could set a proper course. The hut book had told us that we were at the Skrykenvann,[1] twenty miles north-east of the Bjornesfjord.

We noticed a man on skis coming across the lake dragging a toboggan, and hastily took cover. Would he go by, or was he coming to the hut? He dropped the toboggan and

1. *Vann, vatn*=water, lake (cf. Derwentwater).

came straight towards us, so we caught him as he came round the corner. Seldom have I seen anyone more terrified, and it was hardly surprising, for, in the middle of the Hardanger Vidda, he had been seized by six bearded men in uniform.

He was examined and interrogated, and a rather amusing conversation ensued, although the situation was really pretty desperate for us. We could not take him with us, and we could not let him go; nor could we kill him, unless he should prove to be a member of the N.S.[1]

One of us asked:

'Are you a member of the N.S.?'

He hesitated. 'Well,' he at last replied, 'I'm not exactly a member, but that's the party I support.'

I asked if he was quite sure.

'Yes,' he said. He was known to be a supporter of the N.S., he added, but he had never got as far as joining the party.

We searched the man more closely and found an identity card, a pocket-book containing three thousand crowns, and bread cards issued both in Uvdal and in Geilo. The identity card showed that he came from Uvdal, the nearest valley to the eastward.

The boys were now generally in favour of shooting him. He had indeed plainly declared himself an N.S. man. But I had a feeling that he was so frightened that he did not know what he was saying, and that he was professing to be an N.S. man because he thought we were Germans.

He was put to a little test. I asked if his neighbours in Uvdal could confirm that he had Nazi sympathies. This was a question he had not expected, and he hesitated before replying:

'I've so many enemies down there that they're sure to say I'm not a Nazi, just to make things difficult for me.'

The situation was clear. The man was afraid, and had not the courage to stand by his opinions. It was anything but easy to convince him that we really were Norwegians. Our relations were not established on a friendly footing till at last he burst out in dialect:

'Lord, but it's grand to see you chaps!'

The weather had improved, and the wind was decreasing

[1]. Nasjonal Samling, the Quisling party.

steadily. We reckoned that by early morning we should have the benefit of the moon. We cooked large pieces of the Uvdal man's reindeer meat, so that would not reach the local black market this time. Late at night we fastened our prisoner to the one toboggan and set off.

We had brought with us from England enough explosive to blow up the high-concentration installation and part of the machinery. As we had landed so far from our destination, however, we decided to take with us only sufficient for the high-concentration installation. Tronstad had said before we started that if we managed to smash that up the job would have been completely successful.

The sun rose over the Numedal mountains, first copper-coloured and then golden. It was one of those splendid mornings often met in the northern countries in winter, when storms have raged and died down.

As the day was breaking we came to a little flat-roofed hut by the Hattevatn. There were signs of reindeer-hunters having been there recently, and the Uvdal man told us that the hut belonged to a brother-in-law of his. The Uvdal people were always up in the mountains shooting reindeer on the sly.

We decided to expend a little of the valuable paraffin, and stopped to have a hot breakfast. Progress had been good and there was plenty of time in hand.

There were continual indications that the area was well stocked with reindeer. Going down towards Kallungsjaa and the Slettedal, we came upon several large herds. It was good to feel that the Grouse party, even if they had had to wait for us a long time, must at any rate have been able to get all the reindeer meat they wanted.

When we came to the edge of the Grasdal and were about to descend the slope, one of the lads caught sight of a man on skis coming up the valley. We flung ourselves down among the boulders, and the Uvdal man betrayed his alarm even more clearly than before, having no desire to become involved in a fight with the Germans. Joachim beckoned to me to come forward, because I knew the Grouse fellows best. I lay down with the telescope and studied the man in the valley. He was about two hundred yards away, and at that distance, with a good glass, I thought it should be possible to see if he were one of our men.

But I could not say who it was. He was packed in so many clothes that it was hard to get a proper view of him, while a huge beard made the face unrecognisable. The situation was not improved when we sighted another ski-runner, coming up the valley in the track of the first man and a couple of hundred yards behind him. Could the second man be Arne? The only thing that made me doubt was that he should have such a red beard.

The two unknown men went on over the lake, keeping the same distance between one another. They went up on to a small eminence, where they stopped and looked out over the Hardanger Vidda.

Joachim asked me to go forward and find out who they could be. If they should be strangers, I could say I was a reindeer-hunter; but by now I was pretty sure that they must be our boys. I threw down my sack, put the pistol in my belt under my camouflage suit, and set off after them.

Ten minutes later I was standing on top of the hillock. In the soft snow I had come right up behind the men unnoticed. I stopped about fifteen yards from them, leant on my sticks and looked at Arne and Claus. It was small wonder that I had not known them at once. They were wearing what in an English shop would be advertised as the last word in sports clothes; but these were so ragged and disgusting that the boys looked like the worst tramps imaginable. Behind their beards their faces were wan and thin, and their shoulders were bent.

It was a dead still, clear day. The Vidda is so flat from Kallungsjaa northwards towards the Bjornesfjord and the Nordmannslaag that one's view over the country appears unlimited.

They were holding a telescope and each tugging at one end, both wanting to look over the Hardanger Vidda and try to find us. When at last they had decided which should look first, I gave a loud cough and was instantly recognised. We were delighted at meeting again and expressed our feelings as strongly as young Norwegians can.

There was back-slapping, and much strong hearty cursing. We ran down to the lake, waving to the others, and soon all Gunnerside was giving expression to the same pleasure I had shown several minutes before.

But the boys looked ill. Their skins had assumed a yellowish tinge, and it was clear that they had been through a very bad time in the past months. 'Nothing,' Arne said when we asked what the trouble had been.

When visitors come to the house it is good Norwegian custom that hospitality shall be shown, and the boys dished up the best they had in their rucksacks. This proved to be crispbread and a form of powdered milk. On this occasion the guests had more to offer than the hosts for we could offer them dried fruit, raisins, chocolate, and tobacco, 'directly imported' from England only five days before.

The question of what we should do with the Uvdal man now became more urgent than ever. We could not take him with us to Grouse headquarters at Lake Saure, and we did not feel happy about releasing him. It was decided that three men should be left with him in a little stone hut in the Grasdal. The rest of us were to go on to headquarters.

It was a tiring walk through the Grasdal and over Store Saure. The Gunnerside party were not accustomed to doing long distances in the mountains, and we were tired and done-up after walking twenty miles. Nor did the Grouse boys seem particularly spry.

Late in the afternoon we reached the headquarters, Svensbu, a hut at Lille Saure, Jens Anton Paulsson and Knut Haugland receiving us with open arms.

We sent a messenger to fetch the others from the Grasdal. Our unknown friend was sent off with an extra hundred crowns in his pocket, a bag containing British rations for ten days, and instructions to hold his tongue. He would be allowed to go down to his own district in three days. I told him that the King's arm was long – in case it should ever occur to him to pass on to the Germans the knowledge he had acquired. By degrees we had come to regard him as a good Norwegian, and we did not think that he would be able to do any harm after three days had passed.

The time at Svensbu was chiefly employed in exchanging courtesies, with much cursing and inquiring after common acquaintances in England. The boys wanted to hear about Colonel Wilson, Professor Tronstad and many other people they knew. Jens, the only member of the Grouse group who understood the blessings of nicotine for a mountain dweller, smoked continuously.

As soon as the flood of talk had in some degree abated, we offered each other the good things we had in the way of food. To offset our imported delicacies, the Grouse lads had reindeer meat of every variety. As they put it, we could have the meat either roast or boiled, or boiled or roast, according to our taste and fancy. Jens, who remembered my shooting expeditions in the mountains in former times, knew that I appreciated the best part of the animal, and we silently divided a couple of marrow-bones.

I knew from experience how dangerous it is to eat too much reindeer meat when the stomach is unaccustomed to it. I ate too much all the same, and had the same stomach trouble which the Grouse boys said had afflicted them.

They sat chewing chocolate and raisins, and could not believe the truth of this fairy story – that somewhere else on the earth there was food enough. Their eyes shone like little children's on Christmas Eve. They were not particularly eager to tell us about their hardships, but showed us what they had been living on – fish-meal porridge and reindeer meat.

At first, Jens told us, they had stayed in a little hut close to the Mös dam known as the Sandvas hut. They called it the sheep-killing hut, so that the name should not give away their whereabouts. There they had prepared to receive the gliders. There were no windows in the room where the stove was; and they had hardly any light, since to open the door was to let in wind and snowdrifts. As it was, the snow came in through every crack when there was a storm. Their long aerial, made of boards nailed together, kept blowing down all the time.

'But we had good food,' one of the boys put in.

It had really tasted good, the soup they made of dogfood: ten or twelve dried fish which they had found under the drying stage. Torstein Skinnarland, Einar's brother, brought food up from the village from time to time. Knut found a stray sheep with a lamb in a ravine, and these were slaughtered. Jens was cook, and he dropped the cooking-pot on the floor when he was about to put it on the table. The fellows did not enjoy crawling round on the floor lapping up gravy and gnawing bones.

Some of the food they brought with them from England had to be left behind where they landed. For security reasons it had been necessary to drop them some distance from the place where the gliders were to come down, and as the result of an error in navigation they had landed still farther away than had been intended. They had a great deal of technical gear with them, so the plane was fully loaded and could not take so much food and personal equipment. As they had to carry everything, the technical gear was more than enough for them.

The snow had come early in the autumn of 1942. From Fjarefit in the Songedal the boys were to make their way to the Skoland marshes near the Mös dam. But the lakes were not yet frozen over, and the long detours round water hazards made the march many times as long as it would otherwise have been. To transport all the equipment they had to make the journey at least twice, trudging through the new snow with their heavy loads. On some days they were unable to move camp more than two or three miles.

The daily ration had to be cut down to a quarter of a plate of pemmican – about 1¾oz. – a handful of oatmeal, a handful of flour, four biscuits and a little butter, cheese, sugar and chocolate.

It is pleasant to ski in the mountains in the Easter sunshine and on the smooth surface of well-marked runs in Nordmarka, but wading along on skis with sixty or eighty pounds on one's back is another matter. The skis become so heavy that the greatest effort of will is required to force oneself forward another step, and in such conditions the body requires much strong and nourishing food. When hunger begins to reduce one's strength, it becomes still more difficult to force oneself to take that extra step forward.

On the same day as the boys reached the Skoland marshes it was announced by wireless from London that the gliders were coming. So they rigged up a wireless beacon, and marked out a landing-place in the snow. Then they walked about and waited all night. It was the first clear, fine night they had had since they landed. But during the night it clouded over; then there was a snow blizzard and they began to fear that the gliders would not arrive.

Through the wireless beacon the man who is running a

station can hear when the aircraft has located him by D/F. Late in the night Knut Haugland reported that the aircraft towing the gliders had discovered his station. The boys had heard a plane cruising over the landing-place in the snow squall. Then there was quiet again.

It was a gloomy morning when they went back to the hut to sleep. They had behind them a time of superhuman toil. That night they seemed at last to have reached their goal. They had heard the aircraft – and then nothing more.

Next day a telegram from London told them that the gliders had been lost.

After the glider disaster the party had moved to a hut farther up on the Vidda. They were there when in December the Germans made a big sweep. Torstein was captured, and they had no contacts at all in the countryside and hardly any food. They were in full agreement that it had been a depressing time.

Jens had a hut near Lake Saure, not far away. He had walked over there one day in November. The mist hung about the peaks like wool, and the going was bad, he had to stamp his way forward on waterlogged skis. He attacked the padlock on the door of his own hut with an axe and file. Suddenly he caught sight of a swede projecting from the snow close to the doorstep. It was soaked and half-rotten, but he enjoyed it. They had lived almost exclusively on thin soup for several weeks – soup made of reindeer moss with a little oatmeal added.

He forced the padlock with the file, but on the lock of the door he had to use the axe. The shaft of the axe broke. He went on working with his sheath-knife, but the lock would not come out.

'I felt myself growing furious with a dead thing,' he said, 'but my fingers were becoming more and more stiff and helpless. At last I realised that in this case gentler methods were no good. I took my Krag and blew out the lock with two rounds. Those were two of the ten precious rounds I had for my rifle.'

Jens had hoped to find some food in the hut. There was nothing but a handful of oatmeal and a bottle of fish-oil. He could not restrain himself, but took a good pull at the bottle right away. But there was joy when he returned to the others with his booty.

About Christmas the boys had moved to the Svensbu hut, and thenceforward the food position improved. Two days before Christmas Jens shot the first reindeer. After that they had plenty of meat, but they were still badly off for other kinds of food.

Luckily there was plenty of work to do, but it was a struggle for existence – a ceaseless fight for food and to keep the wireless service going. They had to be clear all the time as to what action they might expect from the German side. There was no time to get on one another's nerves, however, and it was quite remarkable what good friends they had been all the time.

The weather had been appalling, and none of them could remember a winter to equal it. Day after day, week after week, the mountains had been a mass of whirling snow. When it became milder there was fog as thick as gruel, and sticky snow on the surface. Even the rare fine days were bitterly cold. Conditions for ski-ing were hopeless from October till far into February.

When things were at their darkest, Jens consoled himself with a couple of lines from Kipling:

> . . . hold on when there is nothing in you
> Except the will which says to them: 'Hold on!'

Claus went out reindeer-hunting. He always wore a happy smile when he came back, weary, bloodstained and dirty, but with a hundred pounds of meat in his sack. Of an evening he would declaim 'lyrical eructations', as he called them, till the others lay across their bunks bent double with laughter.

Arne, who had been fit enough to carry heavy accumulators for miles through fog and driving snow which stung like a whip-lash, crept into bed when it was cold with his cap pulled down over his ears. Knut had been sitting at his wireless set for weeks, his fingers growing stiff and numb on the keys as the weather worsened.

Many times they had watched Einar racing down to Mösstrand to get fresh information. He could also cook food better than any housewife.

They had lain in the dark and amused themselves by

delivering lectures to one another – on 'tact and good manners', for example, or 'the art of shooting reindeer'. They learnt to value the small things in life. 'A lump of sugar, a pat of butter or a crust of bread made us happy', Jens told us. 'We learnt what good comradeship meant. It was a time I'd be sorry to have missed.'

Jens put a few wet sticks into the stove. The stove was hot now, so the wood dried quickly and burnt well. A small paraffin lamp threw a faint light on the faces round it. Floor and walls were covered with reindeer skins, but the cold struck through nevertheless. The hut was damp, for there were too many people in its limited space. Arne stretched himself and carefully took two raisins.

As the winter wore on the Grouse boys had made themselves fairly comfortable at Svensbu. They had to dig up wood from under the snow, but gradually a small dump was collected. Arne had made a trip back to the place where the plane had dropped them, and managed to find some of the food they had left there. They cooked meat and porridge in the evening, so that the food had only to be heated up in the morning. They had a reindeer's stomach lying in the driven snow outside the hut, so that they could cut off large pieces and throw them straight into the cooking-pot. The contents of the reindeer's stomach were green and good eating, and full of vitamin C.

All shared in the work. One went out after reindeer, another in search of wood. Knut might want help with the wireless now and again. Food had to be cooked too.

During the darkest time the sun was quite hidden behind the Sörenhellernut, and the first day when they had a few minutes' sunshine gave them much pleasure. The minutes of sunshine became more and more day by day.

They watched the weather carefully. It might look fine, but dark banks of cloud still hung in the north-west, over the Vraasjönut. 'No operation to-night' was the usual remark when Einar came in in the morning and told them that the western sky was overcast. They knew from experience that as long as the Vraasjönut was clouded over no aircraft would come, for then there was bad flying weather farther west.

The boys from Gunnerside went out for a run on their skis. They had plenty of routes to choose between. There was a track over the Nusstjönn[1] towards the Vraasjö, and another led in over the ridge towards Vesle Saure. But across the ice towards Haalehovd and the Angelbutjönn shone hard-beaten runs; and it was up there that the Grouse party had found the best ground for reindeer.

A short distance to the westward stood a stake marking a point at which meat had been buried in the snow. In front of the hut the snow was stained with blood. A few reindeer skins, heads and horns lay outside. The snow lay high up the walls, and there was a large drift in front of the door.

I had brought a special message to Grouse from the Supreme Command of the Armed Forces. While the Gunnerside party were out ski-ing I read aloud the order about the organising of future work in the province of Telemark. The message was printed on rice paper, so that it could be eaten in case the bearer was taken prisoner.

'Is that food?' Knut asked, as I crumpled this paper up and was about to throw it into the fire.

'Quite digestible.'

'Well, we don't throw away food here at Svensbu.' He took the paper and began to chew. It may have been a bit tough, but the lads at Svensbu were not spoilt.

4. A LITTLE BANG AT VEMORK

The day after we arrived at Svensbu the question of the attack on the heavy-water establishment at Vemork was taken up. The boys at Svensbu had continually been obtaining fresh information from Vemork. Now we all sat down together and wrote on small scraps of paper all the questions to which we wanted answers. The scraps of paper were laid in

1. *Tjönn* (tjern)=tarn.

a heap and the questions sorted. Finally Claus was sent off to Rjukan to get the very latest information. He had with him a list of over thirty questions.

It was Thursday, 25th February. We decided to move forward during Saturday to a jumping-off position as near Vemork as possible. We were to strike on Sunday night. As an advance base, Jens recommended the Fjösbudal, where there were isolated summer farms and huts which were seldom or never used. We were to spend Friday night in a hut by Lake Langesjaa, where Jens knew there would be plenty of good food. It belonged to an ironmonger in Rjukan, but even if he had fitted it with iron doors and shutters, we should get in all right with our explosives.

Knut and Einar were wireless operators and were to be left behind in the mountains. Einar we had not seen at all, as he had been living in a stone hut some way off. That left nine of us to carry out the attack.

On Friday we set off. There had been hardly any fine weather that winter, and again we came in for a storm. But after a short search we found the hut. Joachim had taken care to bring with him from England a large pair of wire-cutters which could go through three-quarters of an inch of iron like butter, and these were now used for the first time. We cut the bolts holding the iron shutters in place right off. Arne, who was a plumber, fell in love with the wire-cutters at once. Perhaps, too, he was thinking of the bullet he carried in his hip, and the wire-cutters which had saved his life during the fighting in the Stryken valley in 1940.

We entered the hut, got a fire lighted, and made a search for what good food there was. Jens was from Rjukan, and no doubt felt a certain responsibility towards his fellow-townsman. He carefully rationed the tinned meat and the one bottle of whisky which the owner of the hut had been kind enough to leave for the King's soldiers.

On Saturday morning we pushed on. With Arne as scout we passed through the Jærbudal with the greatest caution. The Rjukan people have a large number of huts in the Jærbudal and we were afraid of being seen. Nine white-clad, well-armed Norwegian soldiers were, moreover, a sight which might attract a good deal of attention in the middle of occupied Norway.

In the Fjösbudal we broke into another hut and waited for Claus to come from Rjukan with the latest information. He had a contact of his own there whom none of the rest of us knew.

There had been an argument as to how far it was practicable to get across the ravine at Vemork. Knut had local knowledge and had declared that it was quite impossible, but air photographs which we had of the area showed that there was a small wood bordering the ravine. Where trees grow a man can make his way. To settle the matter it was decided to send Claus on reconnaissance as soon as he came back from Rjukan.

When he arrived he had written answers to all the questions we had drawn up. It was not long before he had to set off again on his new commission. After three or four hours' absence he was back again, and reported that it was easy to get across the river Maan and up on to the railway line providing we took the right route. He had reconnoitred this route, which was about halfway between Vemork and Rjukan.

The Germans no doubt considered that Vemork was so well protected by nature that it would be difficult for attackers to reach it. The works lie like an eagle's eyrie high up on the mountainside. In front the way is completely barred by a deep and sheer ravine, cut by the Maan river in its thousand years' journey to the sea. Its waters with unwearying toil have made a perpendicular-sided crack in the bottom of the valley. Across this crack, the Germans thought, no one could make his way. A narrow suspension bridge, about seventy-five feet long, crosses the ravine at one point, and this was kept under constant close guard.

From the bridge a steep, narrow path leads up to the factory. At the back of the buildings the hill is very steep, and was partly covered with rough ice, the only way down it being a long flight of steps beside the pipe-line. The area round the pipe-line was mined, and the Germans had probably laid mines round the fence enclosing the works as well.

To be able to resist an attack in the dark the Germans

had machine-guns and searchlights on top of the factory. They could illuminate the whole area and at the same time floodlight the pipe-line. We were not much afraid of the searchlights, however, and counted on being able to get through unnoticed. The land mines were a greater menace.

In the German defences at Rjukan there was nevertheless one weak point – the railway line which led from Rjukan to Vemork. It was cut out of the hillside and was used only now and then for transporting machinery to the works. Our contacts had reported that the railway line, so far as they knew, was not guarded.

The Germans had a guard of fifteen men stationed in a hut in the middle of the yard between the buildings. We reckoned that from eight to twelve of this force would be in the hut, the others being distributed round the area of the works. One man would be on guard at the bridge over the ravine, another in the guard-room at the entrance. One or two men would be up on the height above Vaaer to guard the reservoir which supplied the power station.

Our plan, as usual on such occasions, was to divide our force in two – a blowing-up party and a covering party. The leader of the operation, Joachim, was to be in command of the blowing-up party, consisting of Fredrik, Birger and Kasper. The covering party, with Jens, Arne, Claus and the Chicken, was to be under my command. The blowing-up party would confine itself absolutely to the carrying out of the task; while the covering party was to deal with any enemy resistance, by force of arms if necessary.

We reckoned that if we managed to post our men as we had planned, the blowing-up party would be able to carry out its task without being disturbed. Once on the spot, we should have no difficulty with the relatively small German force at Vemork.

It was curious that the Germans had detailed only fifteen men to guard Vemork, particularly after the glider attempt. They ought to have known that an attack on one of their most vital military objectives was pending. And with the whole army of occupation available, a prudent general would have placed more men at such an important post.

There was a discussion as to how far we could follow the original plan made by Professor Tronstad. This was that we should go down the mountainside at Vaaer. We were to leave our packs up on the top and carry only arms and explosives. We had counted on being able to make a good track down through the deep snow and use it to go up again. Now we had come down another way, through the Fjösbudal. If we were to go back through the Fjösbudal, following our own tracks, we should have to cross the river and the bridge at Vaaer about an hour after carrying out the operation. We dared not do that; for in that time the Germans would certainly have come up from Rjukan with strong forces and occupied all roads and bridges.

It was possible to go back across the suspension bridge over the ravine, or go down towards Rjukan so as to take to the hills along the Ryes road, a narrow mountain route passing under the cable railway which runs up to the mountains from Rjukan. This road was used while the mountain railway was being built. To go straight up the mountainside without using a road we discovered to be impossible, as there were some three feet of wet snow. We should have become separated before we had climbed the 1,500 feet into the mountains.

There was a long discussion on the two alternatives—the suspension bridge and the Ryes road. At last we decided on the latter, having discovered that the Ryes road could be reached by means of a disused track running up the mountains on the north side and parallel with the main road. Both our line of advance and our line of retreat had now been fixed.

Hitler's order to shoot every commando or sabotage soldier had little effect on us. We had agreed that if anyone was wounded, the best thing he could do was to take a pill and finish himself off.

Finally, the plans having been discussed in the minutest detail, we just sat and waited until it was time to go to work.

We were having a smoke while waiting, when we noticed that some young people from Rjukan had had the idea of making a trip to the Fjösbudal. The next hut, which was not many yards from ours, had been occupied by two couples. They were taken into custody and told to stay in the hut till Sunday evening.

It was no wonder that they were surprised to find Norwegian soldiers in the middle of southern Norway in February, 1943. Needless to say, they received no explanation of our presence, but our mutual curiosity was great. I for my part felt an almost irresistible desire to talk to Norwegians who had lived under German occupation for the whole of the previous year. I felt that they had had an experience which for the last year had been denied to me. In fact, however, not much was said. The two couples were isolated in their hut, and had to sit there and speculate as to what kind of people we were.

We set out from the hut in the Fjösbudal at 8 p.m. Everything we had had with us which could betray its foreign origin was got rid of before we started.

The first five or six hundred yards down the mountainside were very steep, and we went at a good pace. Halfway down we sighted our objective for the first time, below us on the other side. The great seven-story factory building bulked large on the landscape, although it lay between mountains some four thousand feet high. It was blowing fairly hard, but nevertheless the hum of the machinery came up to us through the ravine. We understood how the Germans could allow themselves to keep so small a guard there. The colossus lay like a medieval castle, built in the most inaccessible place, protected by precipices and rivers.

When we approached the high road between Rjukan and the Mösvatn, we found it best to carry our skis. We joined the road a little above the bends at Vaaer.

Claus had reported that the Germans for some reason or other had moved a fairly large number of troops towards the Mösvatn in the course of the day. We were, therefore, rather nervous when we came down on to the road, but we had to keep to it if we were to arrive in anything like reasonable time. The hillsides were so steep, and so much snow was lying, that it was impossible for us to get forward under the cover of the wood. So we advanced in single file, with Claus well ahead as scout.

It was fairly quiet now, and we took a chance of being able to cover about a mile and a quarter along the high road without being detected.

When we came to the bends at Vaaer, we left the road

and cut across country to rejoin the road again by the Vaaer beck. Thus we avoided the built-up area of Vaaer itself.

The hillside was very steep and covered with wet, heavy snow. We waded and stumbled, leaving most of the work to the law of gravity as we slithered downhill.

Three or four of us had reached the Vaaer bridge, and the others were sliding down towards the road. Just then two buses carrying shift workers appeared from the direction of Vaaer. It was only by a hair's breadth that a large part of the sabotage group missed landing on the roof of one of the buses.

When the buses had passed, we assembled in a little shanty on the east bank of the Vaaer river. Thence we continued along the road in single file. There should now be no great risk in proceeding along the road, for it was nearly midnight and we should be able to observe an approaching car from several miles away. The cars in those parts drove with all their lights on.

When we had covered about two miles we came to a small field, and Claus signed to us to leave the road. It was here that he had found it possible to cross the river Maan and get up on to the railway line on the opposite side.

The crossing of the river went with astonishing ease. There had been a great deal of snow that winter, but the Maan is a regulated river. Not even the quick thaw we had had in the last twenty-four hours could bring any undue volume of water into the stream.

We ran across the ice and began to clamber up the other side. In such circumstances it is always tiring to be one of a party. One has a feeling all the time that one's comrades are climbing faster than oneself, and that one must hurry to keep up with them. This naturally means that the others quicken their pace too, and the speed of the whole party steadily increases. It was a wearisome climb before we stood on the railway line above.

The line was not in use, but there was so little snow there that we could easily get along it. It was a dark night and there was no moon. The unusually strong south-west wind which accompanied the thaw drowned all the noise we made. Half an hour before midnight we came to a snow-covered building five hundred yards from Vemork, where we ate a little chocolate and waited for the change of sentries. Although it was mild, we were pretty cold in the wind.

The change of sentries should take place at midnight. Half an hour later we were to attack. The covering party was to advance towards the factory first to force the gate or the fence, if this was necessary.

I went forward, with Arne a few yards behind me. 'Good luck,' said Joachim. We had calculated that the Germans would have laid mine-fields to protect the factory. If we were unlucky enough to come upon a mine, then not more than two of us would go in the first round. Arne and I found a trodden path which followed the railway line from a tool-shed right up to the factory. Here we felt fairly safe.

We went right up to the gate and, with the help of the cutters which Arne had brought with him, it was a matter of seconds to cut through a thin little iron chain which barred the way to one of the most important military objectives in Europe.

Jens formed our line of communications to the rear, and he beckoned to the others. In a moment we had the whole covering group by the gate, and a few minutes later every man was at his post.

We were well armed: five tommy-guns among nine men, and everyone had a pistol, a knife and hand-grenades.

The blowing-up party, led by Joachim, first tried to get in through one of the doors on the ground floor, but this attempt had to be given up and another way found. Joachim and Fredrik became separated from the other two while searching for the cable intake. They found the intake, and decided to crawl in alone. They crept along among a quantity of pipes under the floor and reached the door leading to the high-concentration installation.

There was only one workman in the room and of course he had nothing to say to two armed men. He was made to stand against the wall and look on. Fortunately he kept quiet.

Joachim began to lay the charges. Suddenly the windows were kicked in. This proved to be Birger and Kasper trying to force an entrance. The broken glass clattered on the floor, but the Germans heard nothing; the loud humming of the generators stifled all other noise. Joachim wore rubber gloves so as to be able to work without being burned by lye or short-circuiting. Nevertheless he cut himself badly when smashing the glass panes to let Birger in.

Now there were two men to deal with the charges, and the work went quickly.

'Take care not to short-circuit,' the watchman said. 'If you do there may be an explosion.'

'Explosion!' said Fredrik. 'That's just what there's going to be!'

Fredrik stood talking to the watchman all the time. He showed the man his uniform.

'Have a good look at this,' he said. 'Notice these marks,' pointing to the sergeant's stripes on his arm. 'If you look carefully, you can tell the Germans what an English uniform looks like. I don't expect there are many of the master race in Rjukan who have had the chance of getting so close to an Allied soldier.'

The fuses were set for two minutes. Joachim cut down the time to half a minute before lighting them. The watchman began to look round in bewilderment when he realised that there was about to be an explosion.

'Where are my spectacles?' he burst out. 'I must have them.'

'On your nose,' Joachim said. 'Take him out,' he added, nodding to Fredrik.

The man was told to run as hard as he could. Fredrik opened the door, and he vanished like a spirit. The boys followed, locking the door carefully behind them.

The time seemed long to us who stood waiting outside. The Chicken had followed the blowing-up party as far as he could, and was to see that none of the sentries at the gate or the bridge could come up towards the factory area. Arne stood in readiness to deny access to the sentries on the height above Vaaer. Claus had the task of guarding the road at the point where we had forced our way into the factory area, and covering our retreat.

Jens and I were together. We should, if necessary, attack the Germans in the hut in the yard. We had stolen forward along the office building, and farther along the power station. To our right we had the electric-light plant, and straight ahead of us lay the Germans' hut.

We had expected to meet Norwegian watchmen, and to dispose of them I had brought a box containing tubes of chloroform. But we saw no Norwegians, and advanced to a point about twenty yards from the German guard hut. There we stood, well hidden behind a couple of empty casks. The level humming from the electric generators in the buildings just behind us made it possible for us to talk to one another without risk of attracting attention.

The factory buildings had seemed large from a distance. Now that we were among them, they seemed gigantic. The space between the power station and the electric-light plant was like a narrow ravine, recalling the winding alleys of Manhattan.

We waited and waited. We knew that the blowing-up party was inside to carry out its part of the task, but we did not know how things were going. Jens had a tommy-gun and a pistol. If the Germans gave the alarm, or showed any sign of realising what was going on, he would start pumping lead into the hut. I had a pistol and five or six hand-grenades. The intention was to throw them in among the Germans through the doors and windows.

'You must remember to call out *Heil Hitler* when you open the door and throw the bombs,' Jens told me.

When once we had reached our post, we both became quite calm, sensing that the operation would be successful. We knew that the Germans' lives were now completely in our hands, the only danger being that the blowing-up party might encounter unexpected difficulties inside the factory. The thin wall of the wooden hut was no protection against our automatic weapons. I was reminded of something which had happened earlier in the war. During the fighting at Tonsaasen we had surrounded a section of Germans in a wooden house. There were dead Germans hanging out of the window, and dead Germans lying inside before we had finished shooting the house to pieces.

We stood there, I dare say, for twenty minutes, but to us it seemed like a whole night. What was it like for the Chicken, Claus and Arne, who were quite alone?

At last there was an explosion, but an astonishingly small, insignificant one. Was this what we had come over a thousand miles to do? Certainly the windows were broken, and a glimmer of light spread out into the night, but it was not particularly impressive.

The Germans likewise clearly did not think that the explosion was very important: it was several minutes before they showed any signs of reacting. We had seen nothing of the blowing-up party's work, and for safety's sake Jens and I decided that we must take it calmly and wait a little longer.

A single German, unarmed, came out of the hut, went over and felt the door leading to the electric-light plant. It was locked, and he went in again; but a moment later he reappeared with a torch in his hand. He came over towards us and threw the light along the ground. Jens put his finger on the trigger.

'Shall I fire?'

'No. He doesn't know what has happened. Leave him as long as possible.' Our task was to blow things up, and not to shoot one German more or less.

The man directed his beam on the ground behind us, and once more Jens raised his tommy-gun. But the German turned and went in again. He probably thought the snow had exploded one of the land mines.

When we were sure that the boys were all out, we moved over towards the gate and the railway line. We discovered Claus and Arne ahead of us. We had arranged a password in advance: 'Piccadilly.' The answer was 'Leicester Square.' As Jens and I approached, we heard Arne's voice. 'Piccadilly,' he hissed. We only quickened our pace without troubling to answer. But Arne would not be put off. 'Piccadilly!' he whispered again. Jens and I grew impatient. 'Shut up, for God's sake!' we burst out simultaneously.

'What's the good of our having passwords if we don't use them?' Arne mumbled angrily when we came up to him.

Claus went on ahead, but soon returned with the news that the blowing-up party were already out on the railway line.

When we had gone a little way along the line, Jens asked me if I ought not to get rid of the chloroform which we had intended for the Norwegian watchmen. I told him that I had thrown it away already. I had no desire to be chloroformed myself, and it would not take much to smash a tube to pieces. I had carefully removed fingerprints from the box before throwing it away, for the Germans had taken my fingerprints when I was arrested in 1941.

'Are you mad?' Jens cried. 'Don't you know the use of gas is forbidden in this war? And now you've started it!'

A short way down Joachim was standing by the railway line, where he had waited for us. We told him that the Germans did not know what had happened and that we had every reason to set our minds at rest.

One usually moves quickly in a retreat, and we went a good deal faster than usual as we hopped and slid down to the Maan and made our way across. The river had risen since we had first crossed it; in consequence of the thaw there was now a good deal of surface water on the ice.

When we were down in the bottom of the valley, we heard the air-raid sirens sound. This was the Germans' signal for general mobilisation in the Rjukan area. They had at last collected their wits and found out what had happened. That did not matter much to us. To capture nine desperate, well-armed men in a dark wood at night would be difficult enough for people with local knowledge; for Wehrmacht men it should be quite impossible.

On the main road things had begun to get lively. Several cars rushed past. When the last of us had crossed the road, a car came so close that we had to throw ourselves into the ditch. We saw that it was a large car with a gas generator in tow. On the other side of the valley, away on the railway line, we could see the lights of electric torches moving about. The German guards had discovered the line of our retreat.

Now we had to take to the hills. We moved as quickly as possible on the slippery ground along the line of telegraph posts. With Jens and Claus leading, on account of their local knowledge, we turned off by a sandpit just before the station for the cable railway. After walking through the wood for a couple of hundred yards we came to the Ryes road. The way to the mountains was open.

To reach the mountains and safety as quickly as possible was only a question of strength. We took over three hours to get up the Ryes road that night. With heavy loads, tired and exhausted, our progress was slow. When at last we mounted the ridge leading to the Hardanger Vidda, we met such a violent westerly gale that we could only just struggle along. Just at the clearing, where the Vidda breaks off sharply and becomes one side of a valley, the wind was so strong that we were several times seized by squalls and thrown back.

Claus left us here to look after a private dump of his own. He was to follow us to Svensbu later.

Late in the day, weary and drooping, we reached the hut at Lake Langesjaa. The operation had been carried out according to plan.

5. WINTER IN THE MOUNTAINS

On the Hardanger Vidda the weather remained the same, with half a gale blowing from the west. We slept in the afternoon and all the night. No one could have started a search in the mountains with the weather steadily growing worse, and we felt pretty safe. In the morning we tried to continue in the direction of Lake Saure and our Svensbu hut, but the weather was so bad that we were unable to go more than a few hundred yards.

The wind had blown great holes in the snow, and the flakes of frozen snow which flew past us were mixed with earth and grit. In order to breathe we had to keep our hands over our mouths. The ice-needles tore our faces till our cheeks felt like open wounds.

We turned and went back to the hut, made coffee and waited. If the Germans were mad enough to venture into the mountains in this weather, at any rate they would not get as far as Langesjaa.

In the afternoon the weather improved, and we succeeded in forcing our way as far as Lake Saure. It had become so dark that even Jens, who knew the country, went into a wrong inlet of Saure before he found Svensbu. On the following day the weather was again so bad that we remained in the hut.

Arne and I made use of the opportunity to go and secrete

a small dump of equipment and other things which we thought we could collect later. Arne had learnt by experience how necessary it was to provide oneself with a reserve supply of clothes, shoes and food. What we did not absolutely need when on the move, or could take with us on our further travels when the others had gone to Sweden, we hid with care under a boulder.

Claus should have joined us on the same day, but there was no sign of him. We thought he must have been held up by the storm, and would appear later. He was such a good man in mountain country that Jens was still quite easy in his mind about him. But Claus did not come on the next day either, and we began to fear an accident. On the third day we must move on.

At a stone hut in the Slettedal we put a note in a tin box saying that the operation had been successfully carried out. The idea was that the two wireless operators, Knut and Einar, should find the box and send a telegram to London.

We reached the hut at Lake Skryken after a surprisingly easy walk. When we had last gone that way the journey had been long and exhausting, but that time we had had both explosives and food to carry. It was fourteen days since we had first arrived at the hut. The rest of our food supply was there, and it was there that we were to separate.

The Gunnerside party was to go to Sweden, Jens and Claus to Oslo; Arne and I were to remain on the Hardanger Vidda. But Claus had still not come. Jens had to set off southwards alone.

Arne and I put on civilian clothes, and packed as many of the most vital necessities as we reckoned we could take with us on a fairly long trip. We were to travel across the Hardanger Vidda in a south-westerly direction to weather the search by the Germans which we now expected. I thought we were economical in our selection. None the less our weapons and food and a little equipment filled several gigantic sacks. We also filled one of the toboggans.

Altogether we had a load of approximately 250 lb. This included weapons and ammunition, some medical supplies, a few tools – knives, an axe, a saw and so on – a few extra clothes, uniforms and boots, cooking utensils and a small amount of paraffin. Then we added to this what food we could manage. Weapons and ammunition accounted for the greater part of the weight but we dared not go unarmed and besides, hunting for wild reindeer should supply us with most of our food. We figured on being able to manage a scant living in the three months until the spring, and summer would make the wilderness more hospitable and suitable for human beings. It was not much we took with us by ordinary standards, but civilisation is mostly an accumulation of non-necessities and we felt rich after having packed.

What we did not know was that it would take the R.A.F. nine months to break through with more supplies and that German counteractions would make it impossible for us to get additional supplies from civilian sources.

When everything was packed, we said farewell to the others. 'Give our best regards to Colonel Wilson and Tronstad. Tell them that we shall manage whatever happens. Send us a wire on your arrival in England, and have a good trip back.' We shook hands all round.

The Gunnerside party started on its long and exhausting journey to Sweden. It had been decided in England that they should go in full uniform for then the Germans could not maintain that the attack on Vemork was not a military operation. We hoped in this way to minimise the risk of German reprisals upon the civilian population in Norway.

It cannot be denied that Arne and I became a trifle nervous after the others had gone. There had been eight of us before, and we thought two would be a very small party if the Germans suddenly appeared. We stood looking after Jens as he went across the lake. It was particularly sad for Arne to say good-bye to a comrade with whom he had toiled and starved for months on end. It was fairly risky for Jens to go alone. We could not help thinking of Claus.

Arne and I had decided to go across the Hardanger Vidda and down into my own country south of the Haukeli road, in the northern part of Setesdal. With a fair surface the journey could be completed in five days.

There was a flurry of snow in the air when we started, but the weather was otherwise fair. It was two days' travel to Skarbu where we hoped to find the two telegraphists, Knut and Einar. The first day we came to a small shepherd's hut.

77

The hut was unfortunately occupied by two young farmers from the Hallingdal valley. The conversation between the four of us was extremely guarded, but it appeared that they were reindeer hunting. They had got a small deer but had only five rounds left for their Krag rifle. I advised them most strongly to get out of the Hardanger Vidda as quickly as humanly possible. They gave us some meat and left in the morning. Later on we learned that they had got into a fire-fight with a German patrol and had used their remaining five rounds to better use than for hunting. They got away but the fact was registered by the German intelligence for use later on.

After two more days of wind and storm, we arrived at the hut in Skarbu. We found the hut full of equipment, weapons and wireless transmitters, but neither of the men was there. It was not long, however, before we sighted someone down on the lake whom Arne recognised as Einar. This was the first time I had met Einar Skinnarland, although he had been at the headquarters at Svensbu before we went down to Vemork.

Einar told us that Knut had gone to the Slettedal to look for our message at the stone hut there. When he returned late in the evening, he did not appear to be in a particularly good temper. We heard that he had searched in the snow for two hours without finding anything. He turned and looked questioningly at Arne and me. How had it gone?

'Don't worry, Knut, keep calm.' I stretched myself out and put my feet on the table. Long seconds passed. 'It all went according to plan. Help me draft a telegram to London, and get it off by the first contact.'

There was jubilation in the hut. Arne and I swallowed the last remains of our coffee, and we sat down and coded. The same evening a telegram went off to London:

HIGH-CONCENTRATION INSTALLATION AT VEMORK COMPLETELY DESTROYED ON NIGHT OF 27TH-28TH STOP GUNNERSIDE HAS GONE TO SWEDEN STOP GREETINGS.

We did not want to remain too long at Skarbu, for we could not tell what the Germans might do. Arne and I would move on westwards according to plan. We fixed with the two telegraphists a place where we should meet them later.

For safety's sake we agreed on a 'post box' known to all of us.

If we lost contact with them as the result of enemy action or ill luck a note was to be placed in the post box saying where the group was. It is not easy to agree upon a spot immediately in the wild mountains. Our post box was an old abandoned lattice-work shooting box, and the notes were to be placed in a tin and buried in the north-western corner.

'Now you can bet the Germans are in a fury,' I said. 'And you can be sure that they'll search every corner of the mountains.'

A thorough comb-out of the whole Hardanger Vidda could be dangerous. We had little food or equipment; we had not been able to establish any depots to speak of; nor had we built any out-of-the-way places to live in. If we were hunted we might very soon be under pressure we could not withstand – and caught. Tronstad and Wilson might have been right when they advised against an expedition so soon after the Vemork operation.

'Pooh!' said Arne. 'Those flat-country peasants and factory hands aren't worth much up here in the wilds.'

Knut was to train Einar as a wireless operator, and they would stay at Nilsbu hut, situated on the Hamrefjell mountain near Mösstrand.[1] There they could hide so well that they would be pretty safe. But what had happened to Gunnerside, and to Claus and Jens?

It took us two days of wearisome foot-slogging to get across to the province of Vinje. In addition to our heavy sacks we had the toboggan, which we took it in turn to draw. 'How the hell did anyone ever contrive to make such a clumsy thing?' Arne asked. It got caught in the drifts and threw a ski-runner off his balance at every step. On Sauerflott we found sticky going and fresh snow; every step was hard labour. Late at night we came to a hut in the Songedal.

We were unlucky enough to run into three men from the neighbourhood, one of whom had known me in old days and, I was certain, recognised me immediately. He knew that I had cleared out two years before and that I was supposed to be in England. But he did not say a word. We spent the night together in the hut, but he gave no sign

1. *Strand*=shore (of the Mösvatn).

that he knew who I was. We said we were on a ski-ing tour. The three men were reindeer-hunting, but declared that they also were on a ski-ing tour. Both parties pretended to believe each other. This was a great encouragement to us. If a man could hold his tongue as this man could, it was a sign that it ought to be practicable to carry on illegal work in Upper Telemark.

We had to cross the Haukeli road, and this gave us a lot of trouble. Strange ski-tracks would always be noticed in the lonely mountain districts, for everyone knows everybody else's business. But we had to cross the road, and that was that.

When we came to the Langesæ hut, Arne went forward, opened the door and welcomed me to my own hut. It was pleasant to return to the place from which the Germans had hunted me in 1941. I felt that I had at last really come back to Norway. As arranged, my cousin, Knut Haukeliseter, had seen that there was a week's supply of food for one man in the hut. There was also a little wood. We ourselves had not much food left, and there was not much possibility of getting any more. There did not seem to be any reindeer in those parts.

It had been arranged that one of the boys from the Vaagslid valley should come up every week to see if there was anyone in the hut. To be on the safe side Arne went to the village to report our arrival. It was prudent for me to keep away, and it was decided that only three of the men in the neighbourhood should know that I was in Norway. Two days later we held our first council of war and made our plans for starting the work.

The greatest difficulty in every illegal undertaking is always to organise it in such a way that it is ready at just the right time. When an illegal militant organisation with personnel, weapons, administration and supervision is formed and organised, it is so exposed to enemy counter-intelligence that it cannot maintain itself for very long. The organisation will be forced to use its weapons to protect itself; a fight will start and spread to the whole community – a fight it is likely to lose.

Partisan forces that are not actively and strongly supported by regular units are extremely vulnerable. The worst that could happen would be a premature uprising against the hated enemy. Such an uprising could not be supported for a long time and it could lead to a catastrophe for our nation. When the time was ripe, however, we could – by using our tremendous mountain plateaux – strike against the enemy when and where we wished. The German lines of communications between east and west had to cross these mountains by rail or road and for hundreds of miles they would be unable to protect their flanks. Their front, the only place where they could deploy their numbers and material strength, would be little more than the width of the road. We on the other hand would have neither front nor flanks – because we would have to deny ourselves the luxury of holding areas. Our attacks would have to be aimed at the enemy's material rather than his personnel. The Germans would, by and by, be forced into a position where their heavy equipment would be an impediment rather than an advantage. They would have to use stronger and stronger forces to keep up their lines of communications to supply their garrisons; garrisons that we had no intention of attacking. They would be their own prisoners and a protection to our own civilians because reprisals could eventually lead to reprisals upon themselves.

The main condition was, however, that the initiative would be with us and that allied and Norwegian forces were attacking from abroad. If this situation was not present the Germans could use their own guerillas against our guerillas and sooner or later we would be forced to hold land and areas at a loss to ourselves. In the meantime, weapons and supplies would be brought in by plane and the key members of the organisation would have to be chosen. We agreed that the task at the moment would be to find a place where we could survive, and get a dependable radio contact with England.

Tor Vinje told us that the preparatory steps for an illegal organisation in Ytre[1] Vinje had been taken, and referred us to one of the local leaders, Tor Bö.

We had feared that the Germans would carry out a search in the mountains after the explosion at Vemork, and indeed we heard that they had sent some patrols over the

1. Outer.

high ground between Röldal and Telemark and Setesdal. After a rather superficial scouring of the country, they had withdrawn.

We were also told that the local Nazi magistrate in Vinje, with the only other member of his party in the district, had been out to find the saboteurs from Vemork. They were armed with a shotgun and an old pistol.

'What will you do if you meet these chaps?' the magistrate was asked.

'Arrest them,' he replied.

His companion perhaps understood better what we could do with our automatic weapons. He was thinking along different lines.

'I think the best thing to do would be to leg it as hard as we can, both of us,' he said.

There had been a tremendous 'flap' at Vemork. Early in the morning after the explosion German reinforcements arrived at Rjukan. Reichskommissar Josef Terboven[1] appeared on the scene, and the first thing he did was to take hostages. He arrested ten of the leading men in Rjukan and threatened to shoot them. General-oberst Falkenhorst[2] came a little later in the day and released the hostages. He said that the operation was of a military nature; moreover, he added, it was the best job he had ever seen.

General Falkenhorst severely admonished the guards at Vemork. They were to take off their great sheepskin coats, and must not go about with tunic collars turned up and caps pulled down against the cold.

'You look like a lot of Father Christmases!' the general roared. 'You can't see or hear saboteurs with all those clothes on! Besides, you're up against the most dangerous men the enemy has. They're chaps who use pistol, poison and knife, the one as easily as the other. They're specially trained to kill silently and quickly.'

The guards certainly cannot have felt very much safer after this, even if their caps were no longer pulled down over

1. Josef Terboven was the German political head of occupied Norway, responsible only to Hitler.
2. The Commander of the German occupation forces in Norway.

their ears. The poor commandant vainly tried to explain what had been done to prevent an attack. The Germans had had a warning when the British gliders were shot down, particularly as they had found maps on board the gliders with a ring round the name Rjukan. The guard had then been increased, and the flood-lighting arranged so that all the lights could be turned on by a single switch. The commandant fussed round the general and begged to be allowed to show him how the lighting arrangement worked.

'Turn it on!' the general ordered.

The N.C.O. in command of the guard, a sergeant-major, disappeared to carry out the order. The others waited. They waited a long time. The sergeant-major did not reappear, but no lights came on. At last the general lost patience and went away.

Next day the sergeant-major went to one of the Norwegian engineers and asked where the switch was. Two days before the attack the whole guard had been changed and a detachment of Austrians put in. The new commander had not thoroughly acquainted himself with the warning system.

The Gunnerside party did get to Sweden. They covered the ground in fourteen days – in full uniform. The little Norwegian detachment went over the mountains of Southern Norway, swung north of Mjösa, and vanished into the great forests towards the Swedish frontier. They crossed five large valleys on the way, but the Germans failed to stop them anywhere. The fugitives were not allowed to establish contact with the Norwegian civil population, and throughout the march they lived on the small rations they had brought with them after the explosion at Vemork. This trek over more than two hundred miles of enemy-occupied territory, carrying supplies and weapons, is a modern saga in itself.

Jens also got through safely. Down in Uvdal he treated himself to the luxury of a room in a pension. The local magistrate came and asked to see his papers, saying that it was a matter of routine after the Vemork explosion. Jens's forged papers were found to be in perfect order, and the magistrate had nothing to say. He cannot have known how near he came to being shot. Jens would not have allowed any close questioning as to where he came from or what he had in his rucksack.

Arne and I hoped that the Germans had given up the search. We decided that the best we could do was to make use of the time to reconnoitre a number of routes in a westerly direction as far as Röldal and Suldal, in order to make the necessary contacts.

It was an uncommonly hard winter with vast amounts of snow. The small quantity of food we had brought with us from the dropping place at Skryken did not last long. The reindeer herds deserted us. We had to hunt for the few solitary animals that drifted across the mountains now and then. One day I managed to kill a squirrel with my ski-ing stick. The poor fellow had somehow lost his home in the woods and drifted into these tremendous snow-covered fields. When I ate him, he was just as miserably thin and undernourished as we were.

Our clothes and boots had to be dried inside our sleeping-bags at night. More often than not we had to eat our food raw. Our bodies themselves had to provide all the warmth they needed and did not get nearly enough nourishment.

Arne was already weakened a good deal after his hardships with the Grouse party, and he ought to have had more to eat.

The wood situation also was precarious. We were so high up in the mountains that it was several miles to the nearest bush. We had to dig up junipers from under the snow, a tiring job and producing very little wood. We often dreamed of wood at night – good dry wood. Sometimes fetching the fuel took us a day's march. The wood was fresh and raw. To get it to burn we stacked it up round the stove. We lit a small fire right under the boiler, and thus at the same time dried the wood round the fire.

One day while I was making tea Arne came home from an unsuccessful hunting expedition. 'You've got it nice and warm in here,' he said, throwing down his rucksack. I rushed to the stove. The fire had spread and three days' wood supply had been burnt up.

Next morning we had to go out and search for wood in a snow squall after a cold and meagre breakfast. After walking for a couple of hours we found some stunted birches. We made large bundles weighing about a hundred pounds each, which we thought would provide us with wood for at least a fortnight. When carrying such a heavy weight, one first needs help to get the sack on one's back. Once there, it can be carried for a long time, but if one wants to rest the sack must be supported on a boulder, or else one must stand upright against a cliff.

I started home first and walked and walked without resting. Weary as I was I dared not stop. I got home without having seen Arne. Half an hour later he arrived, with a very small load and very depressed.

'I fell down and couldn't get up again with the sack,' he said.

The bad weather became our constant companion. We dragged ourselves out shooting, undernourished and thinly clad. The going was sometimes heavy and sometimes easy, but the reindeer were always absent and the weather always severe. If the ice-needles were not lashing us in the face, the mist lay over the mountains as thick as soup and prevented hunting of any kind.

Hunger is a hard master. Not the hunger that the civilised person sometimes experiences; he says he is hungry because his stomach tells him that it has room for some more food. But the hunger that drains the strength out of the whole body and paralyses will and determination. A hunter gets into a vicious circle; he needs food to give him strength to go out and hunt for food. Food becomes the big over-riding thought, day and night, that dominates everything – even friendship.

We were sitting in the hut one evening, having finished our meagre daily rations.

'When this war is over, I shall spend all my money on food,' said Arne: 'I shan't spend any on girls.'

'Same here,' I said, licking a dry spoon.

Arne ran his hand over his hollow cheeks.

'I regret the money I've spent on women in the past,' said he seriously.

We talked and dreamed of reindeer meat – juicy, tender, raw reindeer meat. But the snowfields lay there lonely, cold and desolate day after day, without a sign of life.

Sometimes we stood, hungry and tired, on the steep slope above the valley and looked at the lights from the little mountain farms beneath. They were poor people who lived down there, in an occupied country. But nevertheless they did not starve. We had arms – but no food. Some day we should get there, and sweep the German rabble out.

The days passed, and the time was approaching when we were to meet Knut and Einar again. We hoped to receive a drop from England in the course of April.

One morning at grey of dawn we went down into the village to talk to the boys. We meant to go on across the valley and north to the wireless station. It was a still fine day with fresh snow on the ground.

When we came down on to the road, I waited while Arne went up to Knut Haukeliseter to fetch bread. It was half past six in the morning. As I stood there in the half-light, some instinct told me that I had better move out into the snow. I saw that there was a light in one of the farms, and to avoid all risk I stepped behind a birch bush which was about the height of a man. The road was not being cleared that winter and was half snowed over.

As I stood there scraping my skis, two men suddenly came trudging through the snow, straight towards me. I stood quite still – just dropping my hand to the pistol in my belt. I saw that they were soldiers and carried rifles. They came so close that I could have touched them with my ski-stick. But they passed. The dim half-light had saved me.

Now there was the devil to pay! Arne must have run up against some of them too. For safety's sake I crawled a little farther back, right into the snow, and waited. Arne came racing down. He had got four loaves and was trying to hold on to them. We must take to the hills again, he said. 'There's a great sweep in progress on the Hardanger Vidda, and the place is chock-full of troops. There's a state of emergency, and people on the farms aren't allowed to go out.'

We looked round to make sure that no more Germans were coming along the road.

'I sincerely hope no one sees my tracks from Nesheim Farm down on to the road,' Arne continued. 'I only just missed running right into the Germans.'

We were in a hole now. We could go right across country,

get into the Hardanger Vidda and try to make contact with Knut and Einar, or we could go back on our own tracks and over to the Setesdal moors again. What I should have liked best was to get down into the woods. But the people at my farm had told Arne that the whole neighbourhood was so full of troops that all movement was impossible. If we made for the woods to the southward, we should have to cross the road at Bjaaen, and we had no wish to do that.

Eventually we set off along our own tracks, back to the mountains. Fortunately the wind had got up a bit. If we were lucky, the track over the Vaagslidvatn might have disappeared in a couple of hours. Those two hours, however, were valuable. People were not allowed to go out; there were Germans everywhere, and here was a track in the fresh snow, from the mountains right down to Nesheim Farm and back. We set off with heavy hearts. We should always be able to shift for ourselves. But how were the people at the farm to explain the ski-tracks?

We crossed the lake at top speed before it grew any lighter. Several Germans appeared on the road, but not till we were in the scrub on the other side.

We had a tough journey southwards over the moor. To get rid of the track altogether we moved up on to a string of high summits and there found bare ground from which the snow had been blown away. We pushed on all day and the next day too, making long detours, and did not stop till we found a violent gale blowing in our faces.

This gale was the best thing that could have happened. Our tracks were completely snowed over. We crept into our bags and let the snow cover us. Soon there was nothing to be seen but two little mounds in the white snowstorm.

The snow is a good coverlet but a bad mattress; it warms one above – and melts below. Our backs grew wet, we changed position and grew wet again. Our food rations were scanty, but we shared them as comrades do. A piece of raw pemmican was the best thing we had, and that was hidden away to be eaten last. We tried to melt snow with a tallow candle and get a little hot water. We lay quietly out in the snow in our thin sleeping-bags for five days and nights. We did not get very cold, but at the end of the time we smelt shocking – raw wool and dirty sweat. At last we had to move on

and went right over to Suldal. There we slipped down into
a wood and dried ourselves, hiding in a cave in a dense patch
of undergrowth.

We had now run clean out of food and had to get in
contact with a peasant at Nordmork Farm. He proved to
be a splendid fellow and provided us with bread, herrings
and potatoes. Meanwhile the Germans were carrying out
a sweep all over the mountains round about.

One day the farmer at Nordmork was able to tell us that
the sweep was over and the Germans gone, after they had
passed quite close to us several times. As far as he knew
there had been no reprisals farther east. The ski-track across
the Vaagslidvatn had been a nightmare to us for nearly three
weeks. What we had most feared was that the Germans would
burn all the houses in the district – as had happened at Telavaag.

In 1941 on the island of Telavaag on the west coast, two
men from the Linge Company had established a radio station.
They were discovered by radio direction findings. They got
into a fire-fight with a large German patrol and were killed,
but in the fight they had killed three German soldiers.

The Germans decided to 'remove' the whole island with its
five hundred inhabitants – men, women and children – from
the face of the earth. All buildings were burned or demolished,
quays, roads and boats were destroyed.

All men between the ages of sixteen and forty-five were
sent to concentration camps in Germany (thirty-one never
came back). All women and children were sent to concentration camps in Norway. Children above the age of six were
taken to a camp separate from their mothers, to be raised in
the 'aryan ideology.' Eleven men at the Grine concentration
camp near Oslo were taken out and shot.

The farmer told us also that access to the Hardanger Vidda
was barred. We had really nothing against this; for it meant
we should have the Vidda to ourselves. We set off from
Suldal one day when there was a ringing hard crust of snow,
so that we left no tracks.

On reaching the Langesæ hut, we found that the Germans had been there and made a fearful mess of the place.
The doors had been broken open and were hanging loose.

Everything of value had been stolen. But in a place agreed upon we found good news:

'The swine have gone now and you can come down to the farms – Tor and Knut.'

The boys had hidden some food for us, and we immediately ate as much as we possibly could.

'There won't be any rationing to-day,' said Arne.

An hour later we started a second meal. Arne ate more, but it was I who was ill – all over my sleeping-bag.

'I'm not the greedy one,' said Arne.

The Germans had not discovered that we had been at Nesheim Farm. The local commander had come along the Vaagslid road with a horse and sledge to investigate, but he had quite overlooked the ski-track that crossed the road in the fresh snow. The track would have told any Norwegian that someone had just gone by.

The Germans' helplessness in wild country astonished us. But they also seemed entirely incapable of understanding the sign language of the wilds. A mountain-dweller on a short walk will notice much that is a closed book to others: here a red fox has been, here a marten has caught a bird, and here the white fox has shuffled his way along. The Germans, on the contrary, more often than not failed to notice even the obvious tracks which a *man* leaves behind him. Whether a track was five minutes, five days or five months old was all the same to them – if they saw the tracks at all.

Nevertheless we could take no chances. We had begun to learn how important it was to move in such a way that everything could be explained. We found that the tracks we had made the first time we crossed the Haukeli road had been noticed, but fortunately only by people who realised that they ought not to be talked about.

After the attack on Vemork, the Germans thought that there might be quite a large force of Allied troops on the Hardanger Vidda. They had used more than 15,000 men and aircraft in their sweep and had thoroughly combed the area from the Bergen railway in the north to Sörland and the Ryfylke fjords in the south. It was not only the Langesæ hut that had been knocked about. Practically all the huts on the Vidda had been searched, and many burnt. The Germans had even dropped bombs on the Vidda.

There had been German ski patrols everywhere, well as-
sisted by Norwegian police and *hird* men, but the result was
meagre. In places where an experienced hillman could have
seen plainly that people had been living for a long time,
they overlooked the most obvious evidence. Reichskommissar
Terboven himself came up to the mountains to take part in
the search. He went up in an aircraft and had to make a
forced landing at Rauhelleren. He and his pilot had to spend
the night there before they were picked up.

After the war we found a few German papers relating to
this search. I have an operational order named 'Adler' (Eagle)
written and conducted by S.S.-Standarten führer and Oberst der
Polizei Fehlis, the highest S.S. and German police officer in
Norway. This order is for a search in just the area where
Arne and I lived. This search was to be in addition to what
the order called the big operation Hardanger Vidda. Our area
was to be searched by five hunting groups of approximately
one hundred and twenty men each, comprising men from the
ordinary German army, German police, S.S. troops and Norwegian Hird and Quisling police. They found nothing.

But it is interesting to learn what the Germans knew, what
they expected to find, and how they intended to accomplish
their task. The order is very detailed and says, among other
things:

1. 'According to information received there are a number of
enemy agents and political fugitives in the area Suldal-
Bykle-Vinge.'[1]

2. 'The saboteurs and enemy agents are heavily armed. All
experience shows that when they are cornered they use their
weapons unscrupulously. Every possible treacherous trick
is used.'

3. 'If possible all suspicious persons should be arrested. If
anyone does not surrender they should be eliminated by
force.'

4. 'Own losses must be prevented.'[2]

5. 'The units shall be led and conducted in such a way
that there will always be a reserve of strength present to
pursue any escaping enemy.'

Bad weather drove the enemy out of our mountains a

1. Just our area – and my father's property.
2. Rather difficult.

couple of times during those twelve days. They were not able to search all the places they were ordered to. The report of one of the Quisling police battalion states:

'27th March. Extremely heavy new snow. Gales and fog with biting wind that went right through our clothes. Our faces were so badly frost-bitten that our headcovers could not protect us. I, the leader, had to walk without a headcover to watch the compass I kept in my hand. My men were suffering from inflamed eyes, badly wind-lashed faces, feet which were wet, blistered and inflamed; even blood poisoning.

28th March. Snow so sticky and difficult that we had to take our skis off and "wade" through the snow.

March 29th. Met a German patrol that, in four days, because of the weather and new snow, had been unable to search the Haetta mountains.

30th March. Strong gales of snow, thick fog, sticky snow. My men have now struggled for a week. Hunptsturmführer Slibold (German) and four of my men had to spend the night in a stone hut. Collected my force at five o'clock in the morning. Everybody in extremely bad condition due to hunger, cold and frost.

8th April. Parade for Standarten führer Fehlis at Dalen. Great praise for our effort.'

The Norwegian police battalion had covered little more than the area that Gunnerside had travelled after its landing to meet Swallow. The German patrols did even less. They never managed to reach my father's hut in Vivik, but tried twice and were beaten back by storms. Here, perhaps, we find one of the main reasons for our ability to live in these mountains even two to three years after the enemy had established our presence. These mountains take the full force of the north Atlantic gales, particularly in autumn and early winter. We did not find the weather especially bad during the big search. But when the full force of a north Atlantic gale strikes, even the animals take cover. Life can be sustained only by digging down into the snow and attempting to outlast the storm. Arne once spent two days in the snow underneath a big stone one hundred yards from our stone hut. He could not get farther. We learned how to 'roll with the punch' and survive. The trolls of Norway protected us. The

Germans feared these mountains.

We now thought it was time to try and get in touch with Knut and Einar again, hoping that they too had come through safely. We set off at midnight, and went through the inhabited area and across the Haukeli road in the dark. It was a run of more than fifty miles over to Hamrefjell. Our skis stuck in the snow but we pressed on. Now at last we should hear how the others had fared during the great sweep.

It is incredible how far one can go when one will and must. We lost our way in the Skinndal and had to scramble down at one of the steepest places. There was a hard crust of snow, almost like ice, and the situation was anything but pleasant. I had descended twenty or thirty yards when I heard a shout, and down came Arne slithering towards me. I flung myself down, seized my ski-sticks by the discs, and drove them through the snow crust. Arne sailed by at full speed, head first, and disappeared over the edge of a slope. Many thoughts flash through one's mind in a moment like that. One of the first things that occurred to me when I saw him rushing by was: what in the world should I do with the body? For I could not believe that there was any possibility of finding my only comrade alive.

I succeeded in finding another way down, and in half an hour I was at the bottom of the steep descent. There was Arne tramping about in the snow, apparently searching for something. I could not help asking if it were true, and if he really was alive. 'Alive? Yes, I'm alive all right,' Arne assured me. 'But I can't find my rucksack. I lost it on the way down. My skis and sticks are gone too.' His face was angry.

We found the skis and sticks scattered around, as much as a hundred yards away; the rucksack was on Arne's back. He had fallen into a narrow gully of snow which ran down between some ugly-looking boulders. The only boulder in the gully itself he had had pace and luck enough to hop over. It was not long before we were on our way again. We met the boys in the Nilsbu hut, and were all delighted to see each other again. The two telegraphists had almost written us off as killed or caught in the great sweep. It had been rumoured that two bearded men had been captured on the Hardanger Vidda, farther west near Röldal, but these proved to have been two fugitives from Odda. Our friends themselves had been warned of the coming sweep and had established themselves on a summit in the Hamrefjell mountains. They had food, paraffin and a tent there, and kept quiet till all was over.

One of their contacts had told them that Claus had got into trouble during the sweep; he had been taken prisoner and put into a bus for transport to Oslo. He had tried to escape on the journey, but the Germans had pursued him, and the bus-driver did not think he had got away. A report had been sent to London that he had probably been shot while attempting to escape.

The question now was how we should get hold of the equipment which had been left behind at Lake Skryken. The supply aircraft had not come on account of the sweep, and we should have to fend for ourselves till autumn.

Einar, Arne and I went northwards to clear up the Svensbu hut and find out what was left at Skryken. At Svensbu we found everything in the wildest disorder; the Germans had turned the place upside down. But they had not discovered anything.

The snow had melted to some extent. It was clear to us that people had been living there for quite a long time. We found boxes of decomposed meat, and other things the boys had hidden. We also found uniforms and British equipment up among some boulders. We took away as much of the stuff as possible. Einar and I pushed on to Skryken; Arne was to go westwards to Ugleflott and meet Knut again at a hut there.

Einar and I had a pleasant but tiring expedition. At Skryken everything was as it had been. We dug up the things that were concealed under the snow, and hid them under some boulders farther up the hillside where they would be safe. We then loaded as much as we could take with us on to a toboggan and moved off westwards.

We succeeded in breaking into a hut by the Krossvatn. The Germans had been there earlier and thrown handgrenades on to the roof, but had given up trying to get in.

We were delighted at being able to effect an entrance where the Germans had tried with explosives and failed. We dug down till the window was clear of snow. There was

93

an iron bar over the shutter, which we knocked away with an axe; then we opened the window cautiously and got in without damaging anything. 'Norwegian troops don't cause damage in their own country,' said Einar. 'The Germans use explosives on a house, and don't even get inside.'

The hut was so snowed up that the stove smoked fearfully, for there was no draught. Einar got up on the roof and made an artificial extension of the pipe with blocks of snow. When he was getting in again, he fell into the snow-hole which we had dug to clear the window, and entered the living-room with glass and fragments of window-sash hanging from him.

'Norwegian troops . . .?' I said.

At six next morning we started on a hard crust of snow, good going, and were at the Bjornesfjord four hours later. It was a stretch of nearly fourteen miles with a weight of between 120 and 180 pounds on the toboggan. When pulling a toboggan one must keep up as high a speed as possible; if not it stops between each pull and has to be started again. It must glide all the time. When we got our breath on a few small descents we cheered each other on as in a race. It was like a long-distance run in the old days, and the war seemed far away.

At the Bjornesfjord we rested and had a meal, and waited for a crust to form on the snow. Here we saw open water for the first time that winter, and sat for several hours looking at the Nordmannslaag, the ice on which had begun to break up. The sight of running water and the thought that there would be sun and summer again, with light clouds and rising fish, was something so entirely wonderful as to be almost incomprehensible. This was the beginning of May.

It was evening before we went on. We came to the hut at Vollane at midnight and broke into it, having covered twenty-six miles in eight hours.

At daybreak we forged ahead with our load, and after a few hours' hard pulling arrived at the hut on Ugleflott and met Arne. Einar went on to the Hamrefjell to meet Knut again.

We ate and drank and made ourselves comfortable in the hut on Ugleflott. We had a toboggan-load of food, and we found in the hut a few old boxes for firewood. Arne got some oatmeal and pemmican and cooked himself a good big bowl of porridge. He had the misfortune to spill it on the floor, but that did not matter; the porridge was eaten.

Next day we made a late start, and had only gone two or three miles before we stopped. There was something which we had dreamed of but could hardly believe was true. Up on the southern slope by the Songevatn a bare ridge had appeared in the sunshine; it smelt of moist earth and germinating life. We had lived long in snow and cold. We had had little shelter and had been obliged to exist just on what nature allowed us. This promise of summer was like a dream. Perhaps we should not have to starve and freeze for a few months. The smell of heather and moss and wet earth gave us a feeling of well-being. The hills would be clad with green again, the days long and light.

We settled down for the night, tearing up heather and lying under our sleeping-bags. We covered our hands with earth and moss, rubbed them together and smelt the coming spring.

We got in touch with the boys at Vaagslid; conditions in the district were so disturbed that we thought it prudent to get away. Arne and I went towards Oslo, after hiding away our sledge-load. I had some old friends in Oslo whom I was anxious to visit in order to procure some equipment. In Ytre Vinje we looked up Tor Bö, whom I met for the first time. The boys were organised and were just waiting. The situation seemed to be very favourable.

On our way to Oslo we crossed the Totakvatn at Rauland. Arne went through the thin spring ice, and before I managed to get him ashore we had the whole hamlet of Kostveit out to save us. I wondered for a moment what on earth I should say if Arne were drowned. But this time too all went well. We were taken into one of the farms and given home-made aquavitae and milk. In the course of the evening one of the peasants noticed that our boots were sewn differently from the usual Norwegian style, and asked how that could be. I evaded the question by saying that I did not know where the boots came from, and that they were no doubt black-market goods from Sweden. The old man made no comment.

Travel restrictions had just been introduced, but Arne and I arrived in Oslo after a couple of days' travelling by bus, taxi and train. We thought the railway carriages dirty and disgusting. In Oslo we stayed with an old friend, Trond Five, and I set him to work procuring mountain equipment.

I had another valuable contact in Oslo, a man who could get us over the frontier in case we wished to disappear. He was away when I called, but I met a friend of his. I knew that Knut Haugland was supposed to be in town, and said that I wanted to meet Knut Strand (Strand was an alias which Knut used in Oslo). Two days later there was a note in Trond's letter-box: we were to be at a particular street corner at a given time with bicycles. At the corner a girl came on a bicycle and fetched us. We followed her for a little while, and she handed us over to another girl on a bicycle. Then we cycled about the town for a little while, and came back almost to the same place from which we had started. There, at a corner, stood Knut. He also had a girl with him.

We stood chatting for a time, and then the girls began to grow impatient and to look at their watches more and more frequently. We understood that Knut had to go and meet someone else. The girl with whom we had been bicycling drew me aside and told me that I too was to meet someone at another place and that I must go. We agreed to meet Knut again, and parted.

Once more we bicycled about the streets. I wondered who it could be who had asked to meet me. In a quarter of an hour we stopped at another corner. There stood – Knut and his girl. Knut had found out that I was in town and had asked for a meeting with me at the same time that I was asking for an appointment with him. The girls only knew that we were to be at certain places at a certain time. It was a hilarious meeting.

Knut knew nothing more about Claus. But he had just been given a commission by headquarters in Oslo. They had been told that a man out at Lier wanted to make contact with headquarters in order to get over into Sweden. It was just at the Lier ridge that Claus had jumped off the bus. Now Knut had been appointed to meet this man out at Bærum.

Three days later we saw Knut again. It was Claus he had met at Bærum.

When Claus had left us at Rjukan, above the steep drop down to the Hardanger Vidda, he had set off westwards to hide a quantity of things. He was unlucky enough to lose his map – the only one he had. He did not think he could find Lake Skryken without a map, and therefore made his way by train to Oslo via Geilo. Three weeks later he felt that he wanted to return to the mountains.

Claus came up to Skryken, found the hut in which we had lived and went in to get something to eat after his long journey. The place was like a pig-sty; he saw at once that the Germans had been there – perhaps were still in the neighbourhood. When he came out, he observed four or five men approaching the hut on skis. He put on his own skis and dashed off. The only weapon he had was a Colt 32, and that was not much to tackle the enemy with; he must rely on being able to escape from them. Claus was not a bad ski-runner, but one at least of the Germans was better and gained on him. The chase went westwards at a great pace. Claus was not making for any particular place; he only wanted to have the evening sun in his face, so that the Germans would be blinded when firing. Luckily only one of them could keep up the pace, but he hung on like a leech. They went up the Geitvassdal with the German still gaining. Claus had seen that the German, like himself, had only a pistol; so that the chances were even, and the best marksman would win.

'The German soon decided the battle in my favour,' Claus had told Knut. When Claus began to fire at him the German was so frightened that he emptied the whole of his magazine – all misses. At once there was an exchange of roles. The German swung round and sped back towards the others. Claus hesitated a little, but then went in pursuit as fast as he could. Every second was precious : the fellow's comrades might appear over the ridge at any moment. Claus fired a few rounds at the enemy at thirty yards. When he thought he had hit him he turned and continued on his way. The sun had now set and darkness was falling. He was saved – at any rate for the time being.

But the ski-track was a problem; the Germans could follow

it even in the dark. Luckily Claus knew that there was clear ice down on the Vraasjö and set his course for it. It was a quiet, starry night, but dark. Just north of the Vraasjö he ran over a precipice in the Slettedal. It must have been a big drop, for he fell very hard, his left arm and shoulder suffering the brunt. But he had to go on. Down by the Mösvatn he very nearly ran into the Germans, with whom the place was swarming; there was no doubt that they had started a big sweep. He could not take to the hills again with his injured shoulder; he must go to a doctor.

In the course of the day, tired and hungry, Claus arrived at Hamaren Farm. He knew the people there, but could not stay. The Germans were searching every single farm in the district. After getting something to eat and resting a little, he went on across the Mösvatn and down into Rauland. He had been on his legs for thirty-six hours and had covered 112 miles.

There was a great commotion in Rauland; he could not have chosen a worse place of refuge. Terboven and Fehlis[1] had just been there and inspected the troops, about three hundred strong. Mild weather set in, with snow and slush, so there was no question of going on. He knew a country shopkeeper at Austbö, with whom he stayed for the night, but he had to sleep on the kitchen floor; the Germans having requisitioned the other rooms.

In the course of the night Claus invented a plausible cover story and dished it up to the Germans next morning. He said that he had offered his services, as a man with local knowledge, in the hunt for the Vemork saboteurs, and had had the misfortune to break his arm while so engaged. The Germans undoubtedly thought him a good fellow, and let him go to the army doctor to be examined. Before he went in he took off the shoulder-holster with his pistol in it, which he always wore, and hung it from the hasp of the window on the outside wall of the waiting-room. He collected the holster and pistol again on the way out. In the doorway he collided with two German S.S. officers; they were as polite as usual and begged his pardon. Claus was not accustomed to

1. Fehlis was the head of the S.S. and all other German police in occupied Norway.

intercourse with Germans, and he was glad that no one noticed his flustered apology in English – 'Sorry!'

The German doctor had Claus sent down in an ambulance to the inland port of Dalen, from where he was to continue his journey independently. At Dalen he said *auf Wiedersehen* to his helpers, and they parted good friends.

A boat on the Bandak canal was leaving next morning, and Claus was tired. The tourist hotel looked inviting, and he took a room there. But again he was unlucky. Terboven and Fehlis, with their staff, arrived at the hotel in the evening and requisitioned most of the rooms. Curiously enough Claus was allowed to keep his. But all the doors were guarded, and there was no question of leaving. All the hotel guests, about thirty in all, were interrogated. They had to give their names, addresses, ages, object of their stay at Dalen, and a quantity of other information. Claus's identity card was closely examined, but it was certainly quite in order. It had been made out in London.

Next morning eighteen of the guests were ordered to pack their things – among them Claus. They were arrested on a charge of 'insolent behaviour' towards the Reichskommissar. A couple of Norwegian girls had at first refused to have dinner with Terboven, and when they saw that they could not get out of it they had been as rude to him as possible at table. Claus was in doubt what to do. Should he tell Terboven and Co. the same story he had dished up to the Germans at Rauland, or was it too risky? He decided that it was probably less dangerous to stay with the transport of prisoners and then try to escape. He had no desire to accompany them all the way to Grini.[1]

Claus heaved a sigh of relief when he saw Terboven and Fehlis depart. Soon afterwards a large bus drove up to the hotel, and the arrested persons were escorted down one by one. Claus took care to get in last, so that he might be nearest the door. He had tucked the pistol into the lining of his skiing blouse.

One of the Germans evidently thought the loading up was going too slowly, for he gave Claus a kick from behind and made him fall forward up the steps. As he did so the pistol

1. Prison camp near Oslo.

slipped out of his ski-ing blouse and fell between the feet of another German. The Germans stood and bellowed orders, all talking at the same time. Claus was in despair. But, after seeing the pistol, the Germans were uncertain what they should do with him. The orders were that all the prisoners should go to Grini, and orders were orders. Finally Claus was sent off with the rest.

A German sat on guard in the front of the bus, while four others on two motor-cycles escorted it, one ten yards ahead and one ten yards behind. Claus was placed on the floor right at the back. He was lucky enough to find himself beside a young lady from Oslo; they got into conversation and were evidently quite enjoying themselves – so much so that the German guard became jealous of Claus, and eventually he and Claus changed places, a thing that by this time Claus desired most of all.

He felt that the moment had come. They had been driving for ten hours, and it had become dark. They went slowly up the Lier hills, for the bus was generator-driven. But the woods did not come near enough to the road for him to dare to jump out. When they came to the top, however, he had to chance it. He opened the door and jumped out into the darkness, amid angry bellowings from the German in the back part of the bus. Claus fell head over heels in the road, but got to his feet and ran, just as the Germans on the rearmost motor-cycle were about to attack him. Hand-grenades burst round him in the woods, and he felt a violent thump in the back from one which hit him in the shoulder. This time Claus was luckier than he had reason to expect, for it did not burst.

It was dark, and he got right away; the Germans had to give it up and go on without him.

Late that evening Claus came to a small farm, where he was well received. Next day a doctor was obtained from Drammen hospital. Claus had injured his shoulder up in the mountains, and he had broken his arm in jumping off the bus. He was taken to Drammen in an ambulance while German soldiers were searching for him in the woods along the road. He was bandaged at the hospital and later transferred to Lier asylum, where he was placed in a solitary cell as a dangerous lunatic while his arm was healing. Then he was ready to travel to England via Sweden.

It was not long before we got a fresh telegram sent off to London. We had all come safely through the German sweep.

6. SUNNY DAYS

While I was at Trond's in Oslo my father came to the house. I hid behind the door as quickly as I could, and Trond succeeded in getting rid of him after a short conversation. Father left without having discovered me.

There is a most important routine security rule for illegal work – never contact your next of kin. A saboteur brings danger with him wherever he goes. Even if he himself can manage, enemy reprisals will strike at the weakest point, his family. If I had known, however, that it was the last chance in my life to see him, I might have made myself known. A year later the Germans killed him in the concentration camp at Grini.

We spent a month in Oslo, and it was a holiday for all of us. At the beginning of June we were to go to the mountains to continue our work.

We acquired bicycles in the town and went up-country on them. It was intended to start the development of the home forces in the course of the summer. We were to travel about the countryside as if we were ordinary summer tourists looking out for black-market goods.

What we had to do first of all was to secure the necessary contacts. There was already an organisation in Ytre Vinje. In the other districts round the mountains – Suldal, Röldal and Bykle – we had to have new contacts. A great part of the summer was spent in travelling about and interviewing people.

We had a delightful time cycling about the country in the warm summer of 1943. One day when I was at Odda I was unlucky enough to run into a cousin from Vinje. Of course she recognised me at once, but pretended that she had never seen me before. Once I was up at Röldal for a time looking at some German minefields. Röldal was in the west frontier zone, and I had an identity card showing that I came from Odda. The name on the card was Hartmann. I was not particularly pleased when one or two agreeable elderly ladies who were staying at the same place became interested in me and wanted to ask me who I was and where I came from.

'Which branch of the Hartmann family do you belong to?' one of them was anxious to know.

Generally speaking, our experience was that women were well suited to illegal work. It may be true that women talk more than men, but I gradually found that where dangerous subjects were concerned they talked less. A woman lacks a man's ability to use his imagination as an instrument, and she often lacks a man's energy. In her capacity of mother, woman has from generation to generation become more closely bound to reality, and clings in a greater degree to the strictly practical things in life. A man has his creative qualities more highly developed; his mental processes extend beyond day-to-day actualities, whether he is artist, politician or soldier. A woman is seldom a leader in rebellion, but she is very often a much better subordinate than a man. She has no outer vanity to satisfy as regards power or universal knowledge; and therefore she does not tell her men or women friends how much she knows to show what an important person she is.

Arne and I also had time to knock about in the mountains by ourselves. We even built a hut of our own. We knew of a good lake for fishing, some fifteen miles into the mountains, and it was good ground for migrating reindeer also. We placed our hut on a rocky slope, where there was plenty of stone for building material. The place was so out of the way and difficult of access that hardly anyone came there.

The hut was to be warm and give good protection against the winter gales, and there was to be room enough for a wireless station with two men. The walls were of stone, and double, so that none of the stones went through the whole wall. The space between the stone walls we filled up with earth and peat. It was long and exhausting work, but the hut steadily improved. Materials for the roof and overhead beams, doors, windows and interior, had to be fetched from a long way off and carried to the spot.

It was marvellous to be able to do creative work with our minds and hands. We became master masons in fitting stone against stone. And we lived well. There were plenty of fat red mountain trout in the lake. We had to swim out with our nets in the icy water, but the sun was shining. The wild reindeer grazed all around and red, raw and fat meat was a good diet for a hungry body. We had no coffee, sugar or tea. Nor had we tobacco. But we were happy.

The hut was called Bamsebu,[1] after a little elk-hound puppy we had acquired up there. Bamse's mother was from Stubbdal in Aasa; the father was said to be from Sollihögda, but I strongly suspected that he was a sheepdog from Oslo. Bamse was a nice dog all the same.

The summer was fine and warm, and we did not wear many clothes. We again realised that civilisation was a mass of superfluities. As soon as the hut was completed, we could go and wander along the lakesides, haul in fish, have meals, lie in the sun and laze, and let the world and the war go their own way. The long, dark, wearisome winter days, with gales and bad weather, with frozen cheeks, hunger and toil, were far away now. Certainly we had no clothes and equipment at all for another winter, but that did not worry us. Sooner or later, no doubt, the Royal Air Force would bring supplies – and in any case winter would not come before to-morrow.

We learnt something that summer which it had taken Indians and Eskimos thousands of years to understand and adapt themselves to. One can live well on meat alone – but only if one eats the whole of the animal. The hooves, brains and intestines – all that modern man throws away – are the best food. We set less store by the clean-cut steaks which civilised man prefers to eat. We also learnt that the meat should be eaten as raw as possible; just a little heating up, or a few seconds in the pan, was all it needed. Good red meat was what we liked.

The Grouse party had lived on meat in the same way as we did. It had made Arne ill, and he was still run down after the first winter. He was under-nourished, and proved

1. *Bamse* means 'little bear'

to be suffering from beri-beri; the change from the Fannies'
cooking in England to the hardships on the Hardanger Vidda
had been too abrupt. It was decided that he should travel to
London in the autumn, after we had received our first supplies. Einar and I would go on camping out together.

Now and then we went about the countryside as tourists,
talked to people and made plans. By autumn we had the
beginning of an efficient fighting organisation; we had now
only to get arms and ammunition.

That we might still have a wireless station, headquarters
in Oslo sent a young telegraphist to the mountains. This was
Niels Krohg. I stationed him at Högetveit farm in Ytre Vinje.

I shall never forget the first time I talked to the farmer,
Aasmund Högetveit. It was a fine sunny day, and we were
on our way down the farm. We sat down and considered
harvest prospects, and chewed straws. The question I was to
put to him had been worrying me for several weeks.

'Can you take on a young fellow?' I asked him. 'He's a
wireless operator, and would have to set up a station on
your farm. No one but you would know that he had a wireless set. To everyone else he would be a farm hand. You'd
be running a great risk, and if the station were found you'd
probably be shot. But if you can take him, you'll be doing
us a great service.'

Aasmund replied that he would have to think it over. He
came back in five minutes and said that I could bring the man
along.

Einar's station was 'Swallow blue' and the new one which
Niels was setting up was 'Swallow green'. When we came
to Norway with the Gunnerside party, the code name 'Grouse'
had been so much used that it had been altered to 'Swallow'.

The great German sweep the previous winter had produced
no results. They had used strong forces and had – as they
thought – been through the Hardanger Vidda and the Setesdal
moors with a fine comb. They realised, nevertheless, that in
spite of all their exertions there were still people on the
Vidda.

Our wireless connection with England worked regularly,
but suffered from the great defect that we had all resumed
at very much the same times and on the same wave-lengths.
The Germans were trying to find us with large D/F stations

in Germany, and they were also operating with stations in the districts round us. Two of their D/F stations were near Rjukan for a time. It looked as if they had succeeded in pin-pointing us from one of the large stations. One of the Germans at Rjukan told our people that they were hearing us and knew that we were on the Vidda. Closer than that, however, they could not get. The Hardanger Vidda was, and remained, our area.

The thought of fighting worried us a bit. It was a thing to be avoided as far as possible in order not to betray our presence. The Germans would gladly have sacrificed a few men to have us located, and even if we knocked out a German detachment it would mean defeat for us. Thus we had had to keep moving all the time and had not been able to carry out our work properly. If things had gone wrong we should perhaps have escaped, but it would have been worse for the people in the villages. The organisation would have been broken up and the Germans would certainly have taken prisoners from among the civilian population.

We knew that the Gestapo used torture to extract information, and we feared for our friends. The Germans' methods frightened us. We were afraid of being captured. The thought of being mishandled was felt as a deep personal humiliation. The helplessness of a human being under torture must be terrible. And then we were afraid of not being able to keep silent ourselves. We talked very little of this. I noticed that the same thoughts hampered a good many of those in the resistance movement.

Late in the summer of 1943 we had, for a time, very few messages to send. Then we scrapped the regular connection with London. London listened for us at fixed times, but we did not send when we had nothing to say. 'They've gone now,' the Germans at Rjukan said when some time had passed.

Once Einar and I were at a hut in the woods in Ytre Vinje. We had moved down towards the inhabited area to receive a contact from there. Einar had a message to get off; he had just begun to send when the aerial fell down and the connection was broken. I hurriedly climbed a fir-tree, fixed the aerial, and in a few minutes Einar was able to begin transmitting again. London was impatient – where had we been?

Einar had not been sending for long when I caught sight of a German reconnaissance plane flying low over the ridges and making straight for the hut. It began to circle over us. I warned Einar, and he quickly sent a message in Q-code saying that contact would be broken off on account of enemy action and that we should resume in ten minutes if possible. I myself had fetched a rifle so as to be ready for action in case the Germans were up to any tricks. The Storch flew on and Einar was able to begin transmitting again. Nevertheless we did not feel any too safe and took care to move that evening.

When Niels came to Högetveit Farm we had two stations. We moved both of them regularly, and counted on this puzzling the Germans still more than they were already.

Our first parachute drop came that autumn. There had been snowy weather, and the autumn was early. I sat in Bamsebu hut and waited a long time for a plane. The period of moonlight in which the planes should have come was over, and Arne had made a journey of over fifty miles up to Einar's station to get new periods agreed on.

One night while I was alone in the hut I heard the hum of engines. It was September; fresh snow had fallen, and the moon was in its last quarter. I jumped up barefooted and went out into the snow with nothing on but my pants. The plane began to circle round; it circled four times and then disappeared. Each time it turned away I dashed in and put on a garment. When the plane had gone I felt more like crying than anything else. They had come two days late with arms and food and coffee, chocolate, tobacco and brandy – and then they had gone back to England with all the good things.

The next day I was pottering about in the pouring rain, getting in some fishing nets. It was small consolation that the nets were full; we could always get fish enough. Late in the evening Arne arrived.

'Well, how did it go?'

'Go?' I said. 'Nothing's happened here as far as I know.'

'London reported to the station that a plane had been here and made a drop,' he said.

So the plane had dropped the things somewhere or other, and probably fairly near, but without my noticing it. We made a search and found the drop a few hundred yards from the hut, on a spit of land that ran out into the lake.

Half of it had fallen into the water. We got enough to carry on with for a time; then we dived into the ice-cold mountain lake, and at last after much toil got everything ashore.

Some of the ammunition was spoilt, but the weapons were as good as ever. The food too was good, for most of it was tinned.

We had a great feast. Here were four or five hundred pounds of chocolate, tinned fruit, sweet biscuits, jam, corned beef, tea, tobacco and all sorts of other delicacies. We had often been half-starved in the past six months; now we ate till we were almost ill. We could take a bar of chocolate whenever we liked, eat a few raisins or other dried fruits, and I could light a pipe at any time of day. We had got a wireless receiving set for ourselves too. We thought gratefully of those who had included this; if only they had known what a joy it was to receive it.

We were now celebrating in September the Christmas of the year before. We received Christmas greetings, and the King's Christmas present for that year to all the armed forces. Tronstad sent a camouflaged greeting. We were delighted with a letter we received from an English lady. It was headed 'To a Norwegian soldier.' She wished us a really good Christmas and said she was certain that we should be able to celebrate the next one at home in our own country!

We were pleased to get the wireless, but it was really not much use to us; for we had neither time nor opportunity to sit and listen to music or variety, and had to content ourselves with following the news.

It was now decided that Arne should go to England, and he set out for Oslo to establish contacts. The intention was that he should come back in the spring. Tor Vinje, who had been the key man in the building up of the organisation, also left for training in England and was to return later.

I shut up Bamsebu, packed my rucksack full of good things, and moved over towards the Mösvatn. I had had a talk with Einar earlier, and we had decided that it would be safe to stay in those parts.

It was an exhausting tramp across the Vidda. The snow had come, and I had to wade through it over Sauerflott. I lay out in the mountains that night, and had a job to boil a cup of tea with the help of three or four handfuls of heather. We were continually having to go over Sauerflott, and had regular places under some big boulder or another where we used to pass the night.

In the morning the snow lay so deep that I had to tunnel my way out. I had a heavy load to carry, and waded and struggled along, falling into deep holes now and then. It took me four hours to walk a distance which I could have covered in an hour on skis. I reached Einar only after twelve hours of ceaseless toil.

At Vaagslid I found that the Germans had sent another large-scale expedition over the Hardanger Vidda and that there were 150 men at Litlos. It pleased me to think what a hard time they would have in getting down to the inhabited regions.

To the eastward, in the Hamrefjell, there had been a parachute drop similar to that which we had received farther west at Bamsebu. Einar and I were well equipped and could begin our wintering.

Late in the autumn I heard that my father had been arrested. Before we went to Sweden in the autumn of 1941 Björn had charge of more than a hundred small wireless sets which had been made for illegal work. He did not know what to do with them, and we hid them in a store-room at my father's place of business. Now – nearly two years afterwards – the Norwegian combined headquarters had found out where they were. But when they were just going to be collected, the Germans carried out a raid. The sets were found, and Father was arrested. He knew nothing about the wireless sets, but there was a great deal he *did* know – about the intelligence work at the submarine bases at Trondheim and farther north. Now he was at Möllergata 19.[1]

The Gestapo's use of torture was always a nightmare to us when we had relatives or friends in their hands. It was particularly bad when the prisoner had nothing to tell. The Germans never believed that. After the war when we arrested some of the fiends, we found them to be insane and had to intern them in an asylum. What a political system!

1. The main German prison.

Kjela, Songa, Bora, Bjönna and Kvenna are the names of the rivers which flow through the south-eastern and the wildest part of the Hardanger Vidda. Here the Vidda and its scenery are just as they have been for all time.

For once, the tourist associations have understood their own limitations and preserved this stretch of wild country. Tracks marked by cairns, blobs of paint, red marks and tourist huts are forbidden south of the Kvenna.

The Vidda stretches for miles between its watercourses in long undulating lines. The mountains are barren and naked. Rubble and boulders, morasses and snowfields are but seldom relieved by single blades of grass. But it was the very barrenness of the mountains and their immense distances which would afford us the necessary protection against enemy intrusion. Foreign troops had never set foot here during the fighting in 1940. When, in their efforts to find us, they pushed forward over these expanses of mountain country, it was always in fear of meeting resistance, for here they were on ground and in conditions unknown to them.

In the mountains and in wild country in general we always wore uniform. We did so not only because it was practical warm clothing, or because we thought it would make any difference if there was fighting, but we liked to feel that here we stood on Norwegian ground which was still held by Norwegian troops, and that the area represented a free Norway, where the rights of the occupying Power had no meaning whatever.

Bora, Songa, Bjönna, Kvenna – how pretty those short names are! The mountain people gave their rivers names like this as if in defiance of the granite and the poverty. To these regions they made their way when they needed something to support life, and it was necessary to feed the many mouths on the farm at home. The rivers gave fish and the mountains meat and skins; this was a way of life which was far safer than tilling the soil.

Pitfall traps in the mountains have from ancient times been regarded as the most important attribute of a farm. There is an old legend of three girls on Romtveit Farm in Vinje, each of whom was to choose her part in running the farm. The eldest chose first, and she chose the pitfalls. The second chose the fishing, and the third had to content herself with tending the farm itself. The legend exemplifies the value set by the mountain-dwellers on the different aspects of mountain life.

We found old, half destroyed stone huts left by hunters of long ago. They had lived on the mountains, and they had lived well. Could not we with our modern equipment, and additional help from England and America, manage not merely well, but very well? The longer we lived in the wilds, the more we adapted ourselves to their rhythm and tempo.

The modern townsman reckons the day in minutes. A farmer and a hunter reckon the year in seasons; the rhythm of their lives is determined by the seasons, with good or bad going for skis, much or little game. Man is a feeble little creation, and when he finds himself in a region of immense distances and cut off from petrol engines and railway lines, he has only himself to rely on; then strong legs and powerful lungs are what he chiefly needs.

We learned that one cannot defy nature, but must adapt and accommodate oneself to her. Nature will not change; it is man who must change, if he is to live in conditions where nature is dominant.

The time passed in fishing, cooking, wood-carrying and hut-building. We were often weary, but for one reason or another weariness never got the better of us. When we were tired – and we often were – we rested. The modern townsman has presumably never discovered that one can rest as well in a heap of snow as at home in bed, if one has time enough to wait till the storm is over and accept conditions as they are.

Our great difficulty was always getting wood. On the high-lying, tempestuous Hardanger Vidda there is no timber but the small juniper bushes. In summer one can always pull up enough junipers to make oneself a cup or two of coffee, but in winter there is only ice and snow. We had to have wood – and wood had to be fetched from a long way off. We went down to the birch woods along the watercourses and cut down the thin sickly trees which grew there. Thence the wood had to be dragged on sledges or carried for miles before we arrived at the hut. In the mountains, wood makes you warm twice – first when you fetch it and then when you burn it.

I set off from Nilsbu hut one morning while Einar remained behind to get into communication with England. I went up past the Store and Lille Meinsvatn and along the Grasdal at a good speed.

We had had no fresh reindeer meat for many weeks, so, if it were possible to find any beasts south of the Kvenna, I thought I would get some now.

I cut across Ugleflott and up towards Sauerflott in order, if necessary, to go right north to the Briskevatn. It was a bitterly cold day with a faint touch of north in the air. The snow was so cold that the skis would not slide, and I wondered whether I should try to grease them with water.

The stocks of wild reindeer in southern Norway are the only ones of any size in Europe. They are relics from vanished ages, the time when the reindeer was the most important source of food supply in the mountain valleys. The reindeer is one of the animals which have changed least through the ages. It is suited to the wild and desolate places where it lives, and requires large areas to draw upon for food.

Exactly the same geographical conditions which favoured the existence of the reindeer supplied the needs of the great works which we were to attack. Up on the high-lying expanses of the Vidda there were huge areas of water, and this water fell down steeply both to east and west. These desolate expanses also made it possible for us to carry on our illegal work.

We succeeded by degrees in adapting ourselves to life on the Vidda. Not only did we live in the same surroundings as the reindeer, but we came to live in approximately the same way. To a great extent we had to subsist on what we ourselves could obtain on the Vidda. We followed the reindeer on its wanderings, and could do without a house – and without sleeping-bags – even in winter. The whole countryside was ours. A gardener can live on a few square yards of earth, but the hunter needs wide open spaces.

No other animal has man's capacity for adapting himself to different conditions of life. We out there on the Vidda came from a modern community with its cultural opportunities and from a modern community's athletic milieu. It was as though we had thus acquired surplus resources which made it possible for us suddenly to live in quite new conditions.

I sighted a herd of deer by the Ormetjönn. Of course it was in as difficult a position as it possibly could be. Nevertheless I thought that in my white camouflage overalls I might be able to get within range. So, rather audaciously, I lay down on my skis, kept my head down and pushed myself forward across the lake.

It was February, and the sun was already strong enough for me to count on the beasts beginning to suffer from snow-blindness, so that when I lay down on my skis they could not see me in my white clothing. In fact, with the wind against me, I got within about two hundred yards of them. Then one of the cows got up and began to grunt.

We humans seem to have a special capacity for scaring wild animals when we most wish to conceal ourselves. If one goes out and potters about without a gun, one can get within astonishingly short range of even the wariest of wild animals. If, on the contrary, one has a rifle and tries to approach a beast quietly, it seems to notice one's presence more quickly.

I was lying on the ground two hundred yards from the deer, with the wind against me and casting no shadow, and yet one of those accursed spring heifers noticed that there was someone about; and of course she would tell the others at once.

However, I was within easy range and took good aim at one of the deer which had jumped up. Her coat was bright and in fine condition, and I thought she might be a barren cow. But now the whole herd had been scared. They dashed away, flinging their heads in every direction. Distance two hundred yards, hardly any wind, a little sun and a good light – the meat was as good as in the bag already.

My rifle misfired. I again pressed the trigger and the same thing happened. Altogether I tried five times, and each time it was a misfire. Meanwhile, of course, the reindeer had jumped up and were far away. Cursing does one a lot of good – but it does not bring home any meat.

I soon perceived what had happened. As a result of the severe cold the small quantities of oil which were still round the mainspring had weakened it so much that the weapon would not fire.

In the circumstances there was only one possibility. If there had been a herd where I was, there must be many animals in the neighbourhood. There was a hut up on Ugleflott, and if there was no one there, I could break in and thaw out the breech so thoroughly that the spring would be quite clean. I started off, and an hour later I was at the hut.

The year before we had broken five locks to get into this hut. Now, of course, the owner had locked it up again. I pulled a few planks out of the wall and got a fire lighted; then I warmed the breech in the fire as much as I dared, and the weapon fired quite readily.

I set off again, and down by Stæra found another herd. But it takes a great deal to keep metal warm when the temperature is – 13°F. It was the same old story.

Late that evening I returned to our hut, having covered nearly fifty miles. To anticipate any remarks about hunters who could not bring home any meat, I learnt by heart a lecture about people who could not keep their rifles free from oil; for it was Einar's rifle I had with me. Before he had time to say a word, I flung all the gear over to him with a volley of curses.

Hunting is like war in that there is only one standard of success. Either one wins the war or one loses it. Either one gets meat or one doesn't. But Einar was too good a comrade to vex a tired and disgruntled sportsman. With his usual skill in cooking he had soon prepared an excellent dinner. A few days later we got our fresh meat.

Two men living together in the wilds, in a hut ten feet each way, easily get on one another's nerves. It was incredible how well we got on, but we became obstinate and dogmatic in our opinions.

I was out shooting on another occasion, and found game. There had been little meat for a long time, and our mouths watered at the thought of plenty of fresh meat. Shooting deer requires a good judgment of the ground and good field technique. The hunter marks the beasts down, stalks them, and fires when he has come within a suitable range. For two hours I crawled on my stomach in the snow while the deer moved slowly on – always away from me. In two seconds I had aimed and missed. I fired at the hindmost animal in the herd and missed again. So there I stood with my mouth still watering, but with no meat.

When I got home Einar and I had an argument about shooting.

'It's best in thick fog,' I said. 'Then one can creep up quite close to them without their seeing anything.'

'Yes, and without your seeing them. Besides, everyone knows it's impossible to find deer in a fog. You only scare them.'

'Don't you believe I know where they are – and can find them?'

Einar made a face. 'Yes, you've proved that. Only a fool goes out shooting in a fog.'

'Oh, hell!' I rushed out of doors and slept outside that night.

Olav Skinndalen lived at the innermost end of the Skinndal. His nearest neighbours were Jon Hammeren and Halvor Varmevold. These three farmers formed a little community of their own, twenty-eight miles from the outside world.

Olav Skinndalen had a horse, and Olav and his horse worked for us. In the winter, as soon as the going became tolerable about the New Year or in the course of January, Olav put snow-shoes on his horse and began to drive wood as far up into the Skinne gorge as he could. Then he came up to us to get English coffee and tobacco. The wood had to be carried for the last three hundred yards.

When the wind had been southerly and westerly, and Olav thought there were reindeer in the neighbourhood, he usually brought his Krag with him. We could then as a rule enlighten him as to whether he would get any meat or not. We, living up there on the edge of the wilderness, soon noticed when there were animals in the neighbourhood. This was a piece of news which always had to be shared with the people in the Skinndal, at Hammeren and at Varmevold.

It was entirely owing to the help we received from these lonely mountain farms that we were able to stay where we were without being discovered. The least we could do was to tell them when they could hunt. What we could give them in the way of tobacco and coffee and other English goods was so little in comparison. And we sometimes had a surplus. These people had no surplus of anything; but they gave the best they had, and they risked their lives to help us.

On the other hand, we had to do all that we could to prevent suspicion falling on the people with whom we were in touch down in the inhabited regions. Nothing caused us more worry than ski-tracks. We sometimes had to make a detour of many miles to lay a track in such a way that it coincided naturally with the life of the mountain hamlets and the people's movements. By using our contacts to cover up ski-tracks, and by expending much energy in going for greater distances than was necessary, we gradually succeeded in moving about without our tracks exciting as much attention as they had done when we first arrived.

Often we stood dead tired, leaning on our ski-sticks, with our destination, a solitary little mountain farm, in sight a few hundred yards away. But our approach must be made so that there would be no tracks running from the prohibited areas to our friends' farm. We would make a detour of an hour or so to get on to a sledge track or a winter road where no one would be surprised at others having passed that way.

Many wild animals sleep by day and live their lives at night or in the twilight. We came to adopt their habits. The long and tiring journeys in the proximity of inhabited areas had to be made at night. We grew accustomed to going through boulders and scree on black autumn nights. But it was easier to make our way on a moonlight winter night. Our skis ran well on the cold snow, and the moonlight gave us light and protection at the same time. In white clothing we were like wild animals on a desolate ice-field. The unreal, shadowless moonshine on white expanses of driven snow was fascinating in its beauty. Even in the fiercest snow blizzards, with our faces bitten by the ice-needles, we noticed the beauty of the mountains as soon as the moon broke through.

Wireless operators were not allowed to have any kind of personal communication with each other, though it might have been pleasant for Einar to have had a talk with one of the pretty English girls who we knew received his messages. It was Christmas, 1943. On the day when he had his last contact with England before Christmas, we thought he might send a greeting. It was a sparkling clear, brilliant winter day. When Einar had sent all his messages, he added the two initials 'MX' (Merry Christmas). An answer came back immediately from England, short but welcome: 'MXT' (Merry Christmas thanks). They were thanking us for our Christmas wishes from Norway.

On Christmas Eve we brought in some small boughs to make a Christmas tree. We sat indoors at Bamsebu munching chocolate, eating reindeer meat, and using our valuable battery to hear a Christmas programme on the wireless. We had stolen a gramophone from a hut, and we put a few records on; there were not many, but each of us had one or two of which he was very fond. Not long after Christmas we had become so tired of each other's pet records that I smashed his favourite to pieces and he mine.

On Boxing Day we went down to Vaagslid for a party. We were wearing our Norwegian uniforms, and the Vaagslid people treated us with the hospitality due to the King's soldiers. We had taken with us chocolate and other good things, also tobacco. We spent the night there, for the village was snowed up and we could not be taken by surprise.

As the winter passed we had found other things to think about besides gramophone music and reindeer-hunting. As early as the summer of 1943 it had been found that the attack on Vemork had not been so successful as had been at first supposed. Tronstad had said before the attack that our chiefs counted on an eighteen months' stoppage. After we had landed in February at Lake Skryken, so far from our goal, it was decided only to take enough explosive to blow up the high concentration installation. If we did that, the job would be a hundred per cent complete, Tronstad said. But on 27th July we had received this telegram:

MOST IMPORTANT TO OBTAIN MOST EXACT INFORMATION ABOUT CONDITIONS AND VOLUME OF PRESENT PRODUCTION

AT VEMORK AND NOTODDEN STOP WHEN IS FINAL PRODUCTION
EXPECTED TO RECOMMENCE IMI HOW IS THE PRODUCT TRANS-
PORTED STOP WHEN WAS THE PRODUCTION PROCESS RESUMED
END

'Imi' in telegraphy actually represents a note of interro-
gation. For us it came also to have another and more important meaning. Once, through a misunderstanding, it was
taken to be a name for the product about which we were
to obtain information from the factories. After that it became
customary to use it, and this soon went so far that we might
get a raspberry if we did not use the designation 'Imi' for
heavy water.

When demolishing the high concentration apparatus in
January 1943, we had managed to lose about a ton of heavy
water which literally poured down the drain in the floor of
the building. It was concentrations from 10.5% to 99.3%;
equivalent to about 350 kg. of high concentrated heavy
water.

The months of February and March were used to clean up
the damage and to build new cells and apparatus. On 17th
April, 1943 the plant began to produce again at a much higher
production rate than before our attack. After the war, Norwegian Hydro gave me these figures:

	1942	1943
January	100 kg	141 kg
February	91 "	107 "
March	103 "	0 "
April	0 "	0 "
May	51 "	3 "
June	94 "	199 "
July	128 "	141 "
August	121 "	100 "
September	96 "	100 "
October	93 "	105 "
November	117 "	41 "
December	147 "	0 "

The Germans had managed to get altogether about 2600 kg. of
heavy water (D_2O) from Vemork in 1940 to 1943.

The main product at the Vemork factory was ammonia, which was shipped to Norwegian Hydro's head works in Porsgrunn for fertiliser production. So desperate were the Germans for heavy water that when the works in Porsgrunn were bombed in July, 1943, and production stopped for a month, the Germans demanded full production at Vemork of heavy water. This meant that the hydrogen which was the main production, would have to be let out into the air at a tremendous loss. The Director General of Hydro, Bjarne Eriksen, refused to do this and was sent to a concentration camp in Germany for his efforts. But production at Vemork was kept down by his engineers and men.

In November Einar and I had been in Ytre Vinje organising the home forces. During this time we stayed at Bö farm in Bögrend. To enter this mountain farmhouse and talk to Olav Bö was an experience. If we ever doubted the Norwegian people's ability and determination to hold out, we only needed to go to the farms in Vinje and Vaagslid. We felt that those people could endure generations of occupation and oppression. When a farmer with his family and his livestock and his land – which he could hardly carry with him if he moved – felt that he could take part in the struggle in any way, another man, who had only himself to look after, ought to be able to go on taking risks.

16th November was a clear, still, fine autumn day, and threshing was going on at the farm. Einar, who was sitting in the barn and was in wireless contact with London, was continually disturbed in his work by the electric motor of the threshing machine. Then suddenly the threshing stopped, and every man left his work. A hundred and fifty four-engined American bombers were flying across Norway in broad daylight as if no German anti-aircraft defences existed. They began to circle over us and then proceeded in an easterly direction, towards Rjukan.

On 19th November we received a telegram from London to this effect: 'Please send earliest possible information regarding last American air attack in your district.' The information was to be sent by a special contact which had been arranged from London.

To stop the Germans from continuing production, the Americans had now decided to have recourse to bombing.

Altogether the Americans had used one hundred and forty bombers plus fifteen Flying Fortresses in two waves, to bomb Vemork and Rjukan. In Rjukan they hit the Saaheim plant. They used more than seven hundred 500 lb. bombs on Vemork and more than one hundred 250 lb. bombs on Saaheim. The Germans had tried to protect the place with two heavy ack-ack batteries (88mm.) and several batteries of 37mm. They had also stretched wires across the valley from mountain to mountain and in addition filled the valley with smoke from smoke generators.

Three bombs hit the hydro-electric plant's pipelines, but the valves on top in the reservoir stopped the devastating flow of water. Four bombs hit the power station and only two hit the electrolysis plant for heavy water. One bomb hit the suspension bridge across the gorge which collapsed. The high concentration plant underneath – seven stories of concrete in the electrolysis plant – was undamaged. Unfortunately a bomb hit a Norwegian bomb shelter and killed twenty-one people, mostly women and children and one man alone was killed far away in the mountains by a stray bomb.

But the bombing was successful as far as the production of heavy water was concerned. The management of Norsk Hydro succeeded in convincing the Germans that further manufacture was useless even after rebuilding; so production at Vemork was stopped. We continually followed what was happening down in the valley, and wondered what our next task would be.

Towards the end of January, 1944, I went for a trip to the westward, and came back through Rauland. A good many tourists had begun to appear in that district, and I risked going through the place along the road and in broad daylight.

Over towards Mösstrand it struck me that there had been unusually heavy traffic along the ski-track to Kromviki. To be quite safe, I left the route, followed the mountain ridge higher up, and came down to the Mösvatn.

When I went into the house at Hammeren Farm, Jon gave me rather a queer look and asked if I had 'met them.'

'Met them?' I said. 'I haven't met anybody.'

'Well, they've got strong patrols out,' Jon told me, 'and we had fifteen men here not long ago.'

Jon knew nothing more of particular interest. I cut the visit as short as possible, and went straight up into the mountains to Nilsbu hut and Einar.

Einar was not alone at Nilsbu. He had with him a Rjukan man, Rolf Sörlie – one of the contacts he had at Rjukan for information about the heavy water. Rolf had astonishing things to tell us. Milorg[1] at Rjukan was mobilised and between two and three hundred men had taken to the hills. I began to have a feeling that the sudden appearance of German patrols might have unpleasant consequences. But Rolf could not say with certainty whether the Germans were out after mobilised Milorg men. He himself had run into a couple of Germans. They had said nothing, but he knew that they were all over the place, as far as a day's march into the mountains from Rjukan.

The situation was fairly dangerous and could easily become worse. Hundreds of young fellows were scattered about in the mountains with little food and poor equipment, and the Germans were already on the march with quite large forces.

Rolf told us that so many people had gone from both Rjukan and Notodden that there was danger of the factories having to stop work. The only thing he could say with certainty was that the order to mobilise had come from Oslo through the usual channels. After a long conference, Milorg's headquarters at Rjukan had felt itself bound to obey orders.

A telegram was immediately sent to London in which we explained the situation as well as we could.

Rolf was told to go to Rjukan and try to stop the mobilisation in one way or another. Those who had already taken to the mountains must try to get home to their places of work. We were afraid that we should have to set up a base for them and supply them with arms and equipment. The situation was strained enough as it was, and the establishment of a military group of some size might set the avalanche rolling all over Norway. Rolf, who had shown himself to be an unusually hardy and capable ski-runner, was given the best meal we could set before him and sent back on his thirty-five-mile run to Rjukan without pausing for a rest.

1. Milorg=Military Organisation (Norwegian resistance group).

The work of unravelling the tangle took three or four days, during which Rolf was continually in motion. In the midst of all this a new and important matter cropped up, which came to demand all our attention.

8. HEAVY WATER IN THE TINNSJO

On 29th January, 1944, we received a telegram from London to the following effect:

'It is reported that the heavy water apparatus at Vemork and Rjukan is to be dismantled and transported to Germany. Can you get this confirmed? Can this transport be prevented?'

Two days later Rolf Sörlie was able to report from Rjukan that Milorg had managed to come back without the Germans noticing that the boys had been away. The management of the factory had loyally done all that it could to conceal the fact that a large part of the personnel was absent. But Milorg headquarters at Rjukan had had to disappear.

Rolf also reported that what remained of the heavy water at Rjukan after the bombing was to be removed; the transport was to take place in a week. Time was very short, and we telegraphed to London that if anything was to be done we must be informed as quickly as possible.

The situation was difficult. The Germans had obtained very large stores of heavy water at Rjukan by emptying all the containers from the whole heavy water process. There would be quantities far exceeding what had been destroyed earlier.

The most important aspect of the matter was that we should now get a chance of striking a blow at the whole process. Previously we had attacked only the high concentration; now the Germans were going to remove all the concentrations, and if we were able to get at them all, we would stop them for a year or two, perhaps for the rest of the war.

Einar and I were the only people we had with sufficient military training in sabotage to be able to carry out any action: Einar must be kept for wireless communication, and would not be able to leave his station. I must therefore make an attack on the heavy water for a second time – and this time alone.

At Vemork the Germans had taken all possible security measures. All the doors and windows on the ground and first floors had been walled up. A large and well-armed guard had been placed on the spot. To get into the factory at all it was necessary, after having reported to the guard, to go up a staircase to the second floor, where one obtained admittance through an armour-plated door.

A one-man attack on Vemork was out of the question. All high concentrations and all concentrations down to 1% (which is a very high concentration) were drawn into different drums. One hundred and fifty-seven electrolysis tubes were tied together and filled forty-nine big drums. The large number of units made any sabotage extremely difficult. In a sabotage action, time is a limiting factor and one man, or even a small group, would have little chance to attach a charge to all these points, and everything was very well guarded.

On the 9th February we sent the following telegram to London:

'Regards attack on (M) stop Lack of time for preparations prevents military attack on Vemork stop Vemork also very well guarded stop Consider best chance the sinking of ferry by civilian sabotage stop Are we permitted stop Only other chance may be to derail train into Svelgfoss gorge stop Reprisals likely after both military and civilian sabotage stop Answer quickly end.'

How could this attack be carried out? Rolf, Einar and I discussed what we should do. We soon found out that the only practical plan would be for Rolf and myself to go to Rjukan to be on the spot and get as much information as possible.

Rolf was given, as quickly as possible, some instruction in the use of modern weapons and explosives. The expedition started on 12th February. Einar had got a couple of men from the farmers at Mösstrand to help us carry the stuff.

I had decided that it would be best, immediately after any action we might carry out, to go to Sweden with a view to a more detailed conference with headquarters in London.

We were four when we started from the Skinndal late at night. We were to cross the Mösvatn in the dark and go on to Lake Langesjaa. Rolf had been going to and fro for days between Rjukan and the Nilsbu hut, in all weathers and on every kind of surface. When we were approaching Langesjaa, he took command and brought us in almost pitch darkness straight to the hut we had decided to use.

We had to break our way in, and we lay down for the rest of that day. A long string of days were to follow with a new rhythm – sleep by day and work at night.

Rolf was able to tell us that the Germans were trying to camouflage the heavy water by marking the drums containing it 'potash-lye'. At the same time they were taking no chances. They had brought two companies of special S.S. troops to Rjukan, and had stationed a couple of aircraft on a small auxiliary airfield at Attraa near the shore of the Tinnsjö. These aircraft were continually scouting over the mountains round Rjukan, and the S.S. troops doing small arms drill in the neighbourhood of the mountain railway.

The Germans knew from their D/F stations that we were somewhere in the mountains. Earlier they had said: 'We know they are there. We can't find them, but we shall see that they don't do any harm.'

From the hut at Lake Langesjaa we went on towards Rjukan, and came down to the mountain ridge in the evening. We looked for a serviceable hut up on the grassy hillside near Rjukan, where we could count on being left in peace for a few days. We found one conveniently placed up on the steep mountainside, where we felt pretty sure that people would not come on skis. Rolf knew who owned the hut and said he was a good fellow.

This hut was admirably placed in a ravine in very thick forest. During the day we could hear the Germans training their men on a higher plateau, about five hundred yards away.

We had gradually developed an elaborate technique for breaking into huts, and locks caused us no difficulties worth mentioning.

I sent home one of the men who had come with us to

carry the stuff, counting on three of us being able to do the job. The other man was sent back to Langesjaa to fetch some things which had been left behind there.

A tiring time for us began. In the evenings we went down to Rjukan to confer, and in the morning we came up to the hut again to have a good sleep till the next evening. I gradually became so accustomed to the quarter-of-a-mile journey up and down the hillside that I suggested to Rolf that we should get season tickets for the trip.

The three thousand foot ascent was steep and difficult. The narrow path may have given us some help, but in places the mountainside was covered with slippery wet ice to a depth of several feet. Each morning it took us three hours of toil to get up. Downhill, of course, we went quite easily.

Once we had a change from this routine. A telegram came from Tronstad asking if it were true that two German professors were staying at Rjukan. These were two of the Germans' heavy water experts, and we replied that the professors he had been inquiring about were really there. Immediately afterwards a fresh message came: we were to try to get in touch with one of them, give him a greeting from Tronstad and remind him that 'the tough old cock tasted good.' When the German received this message, he would understand that we really were in contact with Professor Tronstad. We were then to tell the German professor that he and his colleague could get off the train in Sweden and report to the nearest British or Norwegian Consulate. Thence they would be sent to England. If the Germans did not agree to this plan, we could kidnap them in whatever way we thought best.

To make all preparations for action was a simple matter. We had weapons, and a car in which to drive the professors away. I went down to Rjukan to try to get in contact with them, and found that they had left the day before.

At Rjukan we had been in touch with Gunnar Syverstad, a laboratory assistant, and two engineers at Vemork named Larsen and Nielsen. Kjell Nielsen was in charge of all transport at the plant, and Gunnar Syverstad had sent us all the reports from Vemork. He had taken care that the production of heavy water should be as small as possible. He had also, with the help of some of the workmen, succeeded in contaminating the heavy water – after a message from us and in accordance with instructions from Tronstad. The previous autumn we had received a telegram from London, the gist of which was as follows:

'It would be of great importance if the heavy water could be contaminated. Oil or cod-liver oil should be placed in the cells. The necessary quantity would be the equivalent of one glass of oil for the apparatus I C 14, or one coffee-cup for a whole electrolytic tube. Care must be observed. On restarting in Germany, the oil will have an effect which can be explained naturally.'

Syverstad and his men had already done their best to contaminate the water for a long time past, at the greatest risk of their lives. But the result was not so good as had been expected. The water was purified again in Germany, and the Germans steadily got more and more of it.

I explained what was intended to Syverstad, Larsen and Kjell Nielsen and we discussed various plans for attacking the transport.

The engineers at Rjukan were uneasy when they heard that an attack on the transport was contemplated. The first thought that had occurred to Einar and me was that this enterprise would cost lives and lead to reprisals. The engineers also took this view.

The fact that the Germans were using the heavy water for atomic experiments, and that an atomic explosion might possibly be brought about, was a thing we now talked of openly. At Rjukan they doubted very much whether the Germans had come in sight of a solution. They also doubted whether an explosion of the kind could be brought about at all.

Einar and I had already discussed the possibility of carrying out an undertaking which must inevitably cost Norwegian lives. We had therefore arranged a telephone code. If I telephoned up to Hovden, close to Mösstrand, and asked if fish could be sent, it meant that our usual contact was to come in and see Einar. He should ask London again whether it was necessary to attack the transport and possibly sink the ferry. If London replied that the action could be stopped, the answer would be that Hovden was sending ten kilos of fish. If it had to be carried through, the answer would be five kilos.

After I had telephoned to Hovden, Einar sent a telegram to London, of which the drift was as follows:

'Bonzo[1] reports as follows: Our contacts at Rjukan think German method is inferior to Norwegian. They doubt if result of operation is worth reprisals. We ourselves cannot decide how important the operations are. Please reply this evening if possible.'

The answer from London came the same day:

'Matter has been considered. It is thought very important that the heavy water shall be destroyed. Hope it can be done without too disastrous results. Send our best wishes for success in the work. Greeting.'

The result, in short, was five kilos of fish.

I called a meeting – Larsen, Syverstad, Kjell Nielsen, Rolf and myself. We discussed the possibilities before us. An attack on Vemork was out of the question after the security measures which the Germans had taken. It might perhaps have been effected by twenty or thirty men from England, but the time was too short for that.

The next question was whether it was possible to do anything to the transport between Vemork and Rjukan, or between Rjukan and the ferry at Mel. Hydro's explosive dump lay just by the railway line between Vemork and Rjukan, where 4,500 lbs. of dynamite were stored. If we could blow up this dump while the train carrying the heavy water was passing, it would be decisive. But the explosion must come at exactly the right moment. That could easily be arranged with the aid of a detonator on the rails. Then there was a guard at the explosive dump, and we did not know what precautionary measures the Germans would take on the line on the day when the transport was to start.

We should need at least a quarter of an hour to overcome the guard, blow open the door and place the detonator. For this to be practicable we should require an exact system for getting reports from Vemork. There was also a risk of the Germans sending a truck ahead of the train, which would detonate the explosive too early. All things considered, there were so many unknown factors that we had to give up the plan.

Another alternative was to blow up the train at Svelgfoss,

1. 'Bonzo' was the author's code name.

between Tinnoset and Notodden. This would certainly be a costly business, and we should have to allow for everyone on the train being killed. The ammonia containers, too, which formed part of the transport, would be a serious danger to the inhabitants of Notodden.

After discussing the matter in all its lights for several days, we came to the conclusion that the safest way was to sink the ferry. The depth of the Tinnsjö is nearly 1,300 feet; the devilish stuff would be safe enough at the bottom.

But could this be done? Was there any chance of placing a charge on board so as to be certain of sinking the ferry? Would it be possible to make it explode at the right moment?

It is always hard to take a decision about actions which involve the loss of human lives. An officer has often to take such decisions in war-time, but in regular warfare it is easier; for then the officer is a small part of an organised apparatus, and his decisions as a rule have consequences only for soldiers, or at most for an enemy population. In this case an act of war was to be carried out which must endanger the lives of a number of our own people – who were not soldiers.

Our contacts at Rjukan were in despair at the thought of the misfortunes to which a fresh act of sabotage must lead. I was the only person who had authority to take a decision. I therefore made it clear that I had full powers to call for help and support in any kind of action. Our orders from London left no room for doubt as to what was intended. It was of vital importance to the result of the war that the Germans should not get the heavy water.

Dressed as a workman, I made a trip on the ferry and found that it took twenty minutes to get from Digerud to Hasleviken, where the lake is deepest. I carried a sten gun wrapped up in a sleeping-bag and a couple of hand-grenades in my rucksack. We had therefore a margin of twenty minutes in which the explosion must take place. But how was it to be effected?

We had no timing device reliable enough to work with, even with the wide margin at our disposal. The only practicable thing would be a clock. But to make a clock produce an explosion one must have electric detonators. Rolf succeeded in getting some through one of his contacts at Rjukan.

One morning after coming up, worn out as usual, from Rjukan, we connected the detonators to an alarm clock to test the release system. The detonators were laid on some pieces of wood, and the alarm was to go off when it was time for us to get up in the evening.

We slept all day. I was woken by being flung out of bed on to the floor. I sprang up, seized the nearest weapon and covered the door. Was it an attack? When I realised what had happened, I opened the door and went outside. Rolf was standing with a sten gun pointing out of the upper window, looking for the enemy, and asked me what had happened. The timing apparatus seemed to be working properly.

The greatest difficulty was still that Milorg was broken up and its leaders gone, so that all contacts had to be made afresh. Conditions at Rjukan were extremely difficult. The false mobilisation order had broken up the top echelon of the Milorg. The rank and file was back at work but the Germans were still investigating. What saved the Milorg was that the Germans had stopped a bus full of young boys trying to get out of town. These youngsters had seen the men getting out into the mountains. When the bus load was taken the youngsters knew nothing else and said that they thought an allied invasion of Norway was imminent and they wanted to get out. The Germans seemed to believe them.

A few of the head men of Milorg were actually arrested but we counted on them keeping silent for long enough to cover the time we needed. The town, however, was getting more and more packed with German troops. I cannot remember Rjukan being more tense than during that week.

Meanwhile, we still needed three men, and we needed a car. Rolf succeeded in getting in touch with a man who was in the country illegally. He had fled to Sweden, but had come back because he was not happy there. Although all Rjukan knew it, he was now staying in the town quite openly. He ought to be a man we could make use of, the more so as I hoped to be able to take him to Sweden with me, for his presence at Rjukan was a danger to Milorg. This man obtained a car for us; he also got hold of a driver, who promised to take one or two refugees out of the town.

What still remained was the most difficult part of all. We

must know with certainty when the transport would start, and we must get the charge placed on board in such a way that it would not be discovered.

Engineer Kjell Nielsen, who was head of Hydro's transport division, delayed the transport till Sunday when we hoped for a low number of passengers. When the transport left town, he was to be taken to hospital and operated upon for appendicitis. He was operated on on the Monday morning, and when the Gestapo wanted to question him around noon the same day, he was still under anaesthetic.

On Saturday afternoon the heavy water was loaded on to two railway trucks and brought down to Rjukan station. Nielsen reported that the papers had been made out for the transport on the following day.

Rolf had a friend who was to travel by the ferry next day. He asked if he might warn him, but after careful consideration we agreed that we dared not take the risk. We could not tell how many friends this friend might have who were in the same situation. I knew that Rolf's nerves and mine would stand the strain, but I could not know whether strangers' nerves would be strong enough for them to let things take their course.

Syverstad's aged mother was to travel by the ferry on Sunday. He was in doubt whether it was right for him to say anything to her. I begged him to keep her at home somehow or other without saying anything, even if it meant knocking her down and locking her in a closet.

Now a new danger appeared. Larsen told us that the Germans were becoming anxious about their precious cargo. Our boys had managed to pick up a telephone conversation from Oslo in which Rjukan had been warned, and ordered to keep a specially close lookout. Obviously the Germans were afraid of an attack by the Allies.

To diminish the risk they decided to divide the transport into two parts. When it arrived at Notodden, half was to proceed by rail and the other half by road. Then, even if an attack should materialise, not more than half the transport would be involved.

We considered the possibilities of an attack on the heavy water while it stood loaded up in Rjukan station the day before it was sent off. The principal difficulty was the great number of points which we should have to blow up. A charge would have to be placed on every single drum, and Kjell Nielsen had said that there were about fifty of them. Rjukan was packed with soldiers, and there was a guard at the station. To carry out a plan like that a large number of men with sufficient training and experience for the task were required. We had to abandon the idea at once.

Rolf and I went over to the bridge which crossed the river Maan and had a look at our target. The trucks had been run up under some lamps, and were guarded. This was on Saturday, 19th February, an hour before midnight. The train was to go at eight next morning, and the ferry was due to leave Mel at ten.

Our driver was waiting in a back street, as arranged. Although we had managed to get him some petrol, he had difficulty in starting the car, and it was an hour before we got away. At one o'clock we were approaching Mel. It was an anxious moment. The engineer Larsen was in the car with us. He was to accompany us to Sweden after the ferry was sunk.

We arrived without any difficulty at a point about three-quarters of a mile from the ferry. There the driver turned the car round and was told to wait. He was to be ready to start at a moment's notice, and if he heard shots he was to drive off at once. In no circumstances was he to wait for more than two hours.

If we had not returned within the given time, Larsen was to make his way to Oslo and get to Sweden as best he could. Larsen was the last of the Hydro's engineers who knew anything about the manufacture of heavy water. He must leave Norway and get over to England at all costs. There he would meet colleagues: the technical head at Vemork, the engineer Jomar Brun, had been there for a long time already. It was he who had helped Tronstad to answer our most difficult questions at the time when we were training for the Vemork operation.

Armed with sten guns, pistols and hand-grenades, we crept past Mel station and down towards the ferry. The bitterly cold night set everything creaking and crackling; the ice on the road snapped sharply as we went over it. When we came out on the bridge by the ferry station, there was as much noise as if a whole company was on the march.

Rolf and the other Rjukan men were told to cover me while I went on board to reconnoitre. All was quiet there. Was it possible that the Germans had omitted to place a guard at the weakest point in the whole route of the transport?

Hearing voices in the crew's quarters, forward, I stole to the companion and listened. There must be a party going on down there, and a game of poker. The other two followed me on to the deck of the ferry. We went down to the third-class accommodation and found a hatchway leading to the bilges. But before we had got the hatch open we heard steps, and took cover behind the nearest table or chair. The ferry watchman was standing in the doorway. He must have left the game of poker on hearing that there were other people on board. The situation was awkward, but not dangerous. We hurriedly explained to the watchman that we had to hide and were looking for a suitable place. The watchman immediately showed us the hatchway in the deck, and told us that they had several times had illicit things with them on their trips.

The Rjukan man now proved invaluable. He talked and talked with the watchman, while Rolf and I flung our sacks down under the deck and began to work.

It was an anxious job, and it took time. The charge and the wire had to be connected; then the detonators had to be connected to the wire and the ignition mechanism. Everything had to be put together and properly laid. It was cramped and uncomfortable down there under the deck, and about a foot of water was standing in the bilge.

The charge was placed in the water and concealed. It consisted of nineteen pounds of high explosive laid in the form of a sausage. We laid it forward, so that the rudder and propeller would rise above the surface when water began to come in. There was also a possibility that the railway trucks would roll off the deck and go to the bottom first.

When the charge exploded, it would blow about eleven square feet out of the ship's side. As the Tinnsjö is narrow, the ferry must sink in less than five minutes, or else it would be possible to beach her. I had spent many hours sitting and calculating how large the hole must be for the ferry to sink quickly enough.

To be on the safe side we used two alarm clocks. The operation must not fail, for everything was at stake. The hammer of the clock would short-circuit the current when it began to strike. The alarm clocks were set up on a rib of the vessel, and a wire led from them down to the charge. We counted on the train being ten minutes late. The clock was set to strike at a quarter to eleven, when the ferry would be over the deepest part of the lake.

Making the last connections was a dangerous job; for an alarm clock is an uncertain instrument, and contact between the hammer and the alarm was avoided by not more than a third of an inch. Thus there was one-third of an inch between us and disaster.

In the meantime the Rjukan man had had a long and well thought out talk with the watchman, and had explained to him that we must go back to Rjukan to fetch some things. We should be on board in the morning in good time before the ferry started.

When I left the watchman I was not clear in my mind as to what I ought to do. He had shown himself to be a good and useful Norwegian. It was very probable that he was just the person whom the Germans would interrogate after the ferry was sunk, and I should have liked to warn him and get him out of the danger zone. I was tempted, too, to take him with us and try to bring him into safety. I remembered the fate of the two Norwegian guards at Vemork, who had been sent to a German concentration camp after the attack there. I did not want to hand over a Norwegian to the Germans. But if the watchman disappeared, there was danger of the Germans' suspicions being aroused next morning.

I contented myself with shaking hands with the watchman and thanking him – which obviously puzzled him.

The car was waiting for us as arranged, and it turned out that we had been away for nearly two hours. Rolf was to take to the hills and keep Einar company while I was away. We said good-bye to him, and the journey to Sweden began.

At Jondalen the car had to turn and go home; for the driver was afraid of getting back to Rjukan too late.

Engineer Larsen and I had to ski through the woods beside the road to Kongsberg. We had a password to use at the ticket office of the railway station so that we could get a book. No Norwegian was allow to travel more than fifteen miles from his home. A German troop train came in and the place was swarming with the green vermin.

Ing Larsen grabbed me by the arm:

'There is the chief of Gestapo in Rjukan and I am not allowed outside the town.'

Larsen locked himself inside one of the toilets. The train that our Gestapo chief was on should link up with the ferry on its way back to Rjukan – the ferry with the heavy water and its explosive charge. There went a fellow who would not be in Rjukan the next day.

Halfway between Hokksund and Drammen I looked at my watch; it was a quarter to eleven. If everything had gone according to plan the ferry should just be sinking; the heavy water would be done for and the Germans' last chance of having it for their atomic experiments would have gone. It had cost us immense toil. We had been maintaining ourselves in the wilds of the Hardanger Vidda for nearly a year and a half. Snow and cold had been our constant companions, and we had carried danger with us wherever we went. Our best friends in Rauland and Vinje had not known what important work they were doing when they helped us. The certainty that a mistake on our part would bring death and destruction on many districts had been a heavy burden to us; for the Germans would have shown no mercy if they had found out who our helpers were.

What would happen now at Rjukan? How many Norwegian lives would be lost through this piece of devilry? The explosion on board the ferry must cost lives, and the reprisals at Rjukan certainly no fewer. Larsen and I did not talk much on the journey. I was thinking of the past.

The English had sacrificed forty-five men with the gliders. Those men had known they would not be able to get away after they had done their work. The bombing had cost twenty-two lives. How many would it be this time? I was glad to know that one of those who were most in the danger zone at Rjukan would probably escape, engineer Kjell Nielsen.

To be on the safe side, Rolf had given me a contact on Heröya, whence the heavy water was to be shipped to Germany. If anything had gone wrong I could take up the work again there. But I found that London too had been prepared for a hitch. Without my knowing it they had sent another sabotage party to Heröya to attack the transport there if we should fail. Submarines were lying in wait in the Skagerak. In Oslo we stayed with Trond as usual.

It was in the paper on Monday evening:

RAILWAY FERRY *Hydro* SUNK IN THE TINNSJO

This was the headline on every front page. The ferry had sunk in a few minutes and was lying in deep water.

Fourteen Norwegians and four Germans had gone down with her, although the captain, who survived the sinking, later reckoned the German loss to be over twenty.

The ferry had carried altogether 14,886,17 kilos of 'potash lye'. Concentrated down, it would be 607 kilos of high concentrated heavy water (see footnote).

Drum No.				
„ „	1:	46,44 · 99,34% =	46,00 kg	
„ „	2:	46,28 · 96,90% =	44,80 „	
„ „	3:	47,57 · 88,10% =	42,00 „	
„ „	4:	45,29 · 75,4 % =	34,10 „	
„ „	5:	45,79 · 67,2 % =	30,80	= 197,70 kg
„ „	6:	90,28 · 46,5 % =		42,00 „
„ „	7:	139,48 · 29,0 % =		40,50 „
„ „	8:	199,0 · 19,5 % =		38,80 „
„ „	9:	185,39 · 14,0 % =		26,00 „
„ „	10:	144,15 · 10,5 % =		15,20 „
„ „	11:	95,2 · 9,0 % =		8,60 „
„ „	12—14:	1046,2 · 6,5 % =		68,00 „
„ „	15—17:	1000,1 · 3,5 % =		35,00 „
„ „	18—23:	2865 · 2,2 % =		52,20 „
„ „	24—29:	2290 · 1,5 % =		34,40 „
„ „	30—39:	3750 · 1,0 % =		37,50 „
„ „	40—49:	3350 · 0,9 % =		30,20 „

$$626,10 \text{ kg} \div 3\%$$
$$\text{Concentrated heavy water} = 607 \text{ kg}$$

Larsen and I continued our escape. We left the train outside Oslo. The Oslo central station was a bad place where the Germans used to search all passengers. At the same time all German higher officials again concentrated at Rjukan. The High Commissioner, J. Terboren and Generaloberst Falkenhorst, with his staff, took a trip out on Tinnsjö lake on board another ferry.

There was nothing they could do now.

As the papers had told us that the blowing-up of the ferry on the Tinnsjö had been successful, Larsen and I carried on to Sweden. After an exhausting three days' journey by way of Nordre Finnskogen we crossed over to the other side of the frontier. For me it was the third time since the beginning of the war.

In Stockholm I was very well received by 'Auntie' at the British Legation. 'Auntie' was a Bergen girl whose function it was to look after the Norwegians in Stockholm. Many of the boys from the Linge Company were there, waiting for new tasks, or resting. It was pleasant to meet comrades from Scotland.

Two days after Larsen and I arrived, Syverstad followed us. He was nervous and harassed; the Tinnsjö tragedy had left a deep imprint on him.

Stockholm was a city without black-out – with neon signs and shop windows full of good things. I went about the streets like most of the other refugees, as delighted as a child at the sight of the lovely things which were displayed. It was quite incredible that they could be not only seen but bought.

It was a real experience to be able to go into a restaurant, order a meal and have it served on a white cloth by a polite waiter. One could choose the dishes one wanted, without first having to carry wood, light the stove and do the cooking. I felt like a polar traveller returned after several years beyond the pale of civilisation. Clean clothes every day and a bath whenever one wanted it – it was like a fairy story.

There was no lack of friendliness in the Swedes, but we never seemed to understand one another during the war. It was pleasant to be received hospitably, but we Norwegians could not bear compassion.

Our feeling of shame at having been beaten in the field made us extremely sensitive to any remark which could be taken to have a derogatory significance; and we made up for this by a certain amount of brag. The Swedes, for their part, might feel the greatest sympathy for Norway, but the feeling was obviously mingled with some annoyance at our having let the western part of the Scandinavian peninsula be overrun by foreign troops and thereby exposed them to danger and unpleasantness.

The Swedes seemed to us to look upon the war as an athletic contest in which they could cheer on one side, but preferably not so loud as to offend the other.

The Norwegians found many friends in Sweden during the war. The people who lived near the frontier were usually splendid. But the farther we got from the frontier the harder it was for us to understand one another. To us the war was in bitter earnest, and we had not the patience to explain that.

'The Germans torture their political prisoners in Norway don't they?' a Stockholm man asked me. We were in a first-class restaurant.

'What do you know about that?'

'There was something about it the other day in some of our more radical papers,' said the Swede.

'Oh,' said I.

The British had made arrangements which enabled us to relax completely in Stockholm. I was given, practically speaking, as much money as I wanted for amusement and for purchases of daily necessities and luxury goods. Now, too, I must dress properly, and was given *carte blanche* to buy things in one of the Stockholm shops. I was ragged and dirty, and did not give the impression of belonging to the class of customer to whom a shopman bows twice. After a couple of hours spent in making purchases, however, the heads of departments began to take an interest in my threadbare person. At this stage I was buying toilet articles, and at last the question of pyjamas arose. Then the head salesman said, addressing me as 'Director':

'Won't you have these? They're dearer.'

The boys did not save the money that was placed at their disposal, but lived a merry, expensive life. We did not know how long we should live, and it was wonderful to be able to enjoy the pleasures of life while there was yet time. I had the impression that the head waiter at one of the city's best restaurants began to practise his formal Swedish bow when he saw me in the street below. I asked after many of the boys, but in all too many cases the answer I received was: 'He's dead. Didn't you know that?'

1943 had been a black year for the Linge Company: we had lost so many men that I could not find out about them all. Several of my best friends were dead. They had gone down fighting in drifters, or had been shot in encounters with the Germans. Many had been wounded, and died after having been in German hands for a long time. What that meant we could only imagine. Of about 110 men forty had lost their lives in the course of a year.

We often discussed the causes of our being in our present situation – having to do our fighting from abroad and live in our own country as outlaws. We always arrived at the same conclusion: if we had been prepared in 1940, if the Norwegian armed forces had had a chance in battle, this would never have happened. We were sure that the Norwegian people had now learned their lesson, and that we should maintain our defences in future. It had been an expensive lesson. German troops had the population of Norway in their power; our best comrades filled the prisons and were being tortured and murdered by men of an alien race.

Colonel Oeen had come over from England on a visit, and he sketched for us some of the new duties which awaited us. It was the winter of 1943-4, and many expected that the Germans would enlist a large part of the Norwegian youth for labour, and later, perhaps, send them to the front. Oeen indicated the possibility of camps having to be established in the mountains or the forests to help the boys who got into difficulties of this kind.

After a fortnight in Stockholm I was thoroughly tired of being there, and longed to get back to the mountains and our comrades in Norway. It was decided that Max Manus,[1] the 'Angel' (Normann Gabrielsen) and I should make the journey back together. We reached Oslo after a fairly exhausting journey – eight days from the frontier into town. Eight days was something of a record, even in spring when the going was heavy, and was probably due in part to our all having kept late hours in Stockholm.

The last leg of our journey took us across the river Glomma, about twenty-five miles east of Oslo. We tried to find a

1. Max Manus: see *Underwater Saboteur*, Fontana.

boat but were unsuccessful. The Germans had their main line of control of all traffic on this broad river and had collected all the boats. I suggested building a float for our rucksacks and swimming for it, but Max suddenly disappeared and came back with – a taxi.

Max had told the taxi driver that we had been foraging for black-market food around the countryside and wanted to go back to Oslo. The driver told us that he had a special permit to cross on one of the big bridges and that the German guards knew his car. He told us that the checkpoint was on the Oslo side of the bridge and that the guards only rarely checked his passengers because they knew him. We decided to travel to Oslo in style.

When the taxi was halfway across the bridge, we pulled out our pistols and primed a couple of hand-grenades. The driver nearly fell out of the car. I gave him a pistol in the side and told him: 'Concentrate on the driving, leave the shooting to us, and don't look so damn scared.' We were waved on at the guard house and paid the driver handsomely when we left him in Oslo.

In Oslo I met Rolf, who was on his way to Stockholm Einar, he told me, was up in Vinje waiting for me to come back. We stayed with Trond as usual. I made arrangements with him for a quantity of supplies to be taken to the mountains.

The Linge Company's Oslo gang arranged for me to be driven up to the mountains in style, disguised as a traveller for the Askim rubber goods factory. My driver was one of the heads of the factory.

As it happened, this man had found out that morning that the Germans were controlling all traffic at Hokksund, as someone had made an unsuccessful attempt to blow up a bridge at Geithus. I had wireless parts with me, as well as new wireless plans and a good deal more illicit stuff, and had no desire to be searched. We therefore decided to drive round Holmestrand.

Nevertheless we had to be prepared for trouble. My driver was therefore given a pistol and five minutes' instruction in the use of the weapon. He then considered himself well equipped and trained to shoot Germans, if this should be necessary. We arrived safely in Vinje after a quiet and peaceful journey.

In the mountains everything was as I remembered. Einar's wireless traffic had become a little slacker. But the home forces were gradually beginning to take shape. Niels Krohg had worked harder all the winter as a farm hand than as a telegraphist, though now he was receiving more frequent messages.

The whole of the illegal work had been extended, and we needed more men. Tor Bö joined us in the mountains. He had a post in the food office, and before he fled he laid his hands on all the ration cards he could find.

The summer passed quietly. But Nilsbu had become by degrees a difficult place to live in, more and more people came to know of it. We decided to build another hut in the Hamrefjell mountains – one which no one should know about. Einar arranged with Olav Skinndalen that the latter should build an extension to his barn. The timber for our hut was driven up with his materials.

The hut was not designed to measure more than ten feet each way. It was to give shelter and warmth to three men. But it is extraordinary how heavy a little hut like that can be when it has to be carried for three hundred yards uphill. We carried and worked for about a fortnight. It was a precipitous ascent, but the materials arrived and the hut was built. Those were fine warm days, but with the warmth came the midges, and it was when we had our hands full that millions of midges took the chance of a meal. I began to understand the man who some years before had gone mad after getting into swarms of midges on Mösstrand.

Tor Bö was a carpenter. Einar, who was a handy-man, could also build a hut. The only and constant hindrance to our plans was Bamse. The tiny puppy which had been Einar's and my pet at Bamsebu had grown large and heavy. One could never be sure that he would not one day take an illicit trip down to the village in search of girl-friends.

We called the hut Skriubu.[1]

Late in the summer Trond and his wife came into the

1. It means 'avalanche-hut'. It was placed in a small valley named Avalanche Valley.

mountains to tell me that my father had died in Grini. The Germans had not been able to make him talk. It had, then, been my last sight of him, that time at Trond's in Oslo when I had been forced to hide behind the door to prevent him discovering that I was there.

There was a steady demand for good telegraphists and, as Trond's wife was anxious to help in some way, I proposed that she should learn this job. She began her training with Einar as instructor.

One day in September a telegram came from London, reading like this:

'To Einar. Large party of eight or ten men including many acquaintances arrives in the moon period about the 1st. Headquarters of two or three men will be with you, with yourself as wireless operator, if you think this is safe.'

One day when we had gone out to meet some of the fellows from Rjukan, we were handed a bundle of identity cards. They came from Oslo and were the so-called 'genuine' faked cards. Name and number were the same as those in the police archives; the photograph was false. When we saw them, we had a pleasant half-hour and a good laugh. There were three of the Grouse boys – Jens, Arne and Claus. There were also cards with photographs of Syverstad and Tronstad, and two of men whom I did not know. So the good old friends were to reassemble by degrees. Evidently they were coming in quickly: London was more than willing to send aircraft with large quantities of material. We pushed on as hard as possible with the work on the home forces.

New landing-grounds for parachute drops were established. These were given code names and marked on the map, and information about them was telegraphed over to England. Then London sent out special messages giving notice of drops at every one of the places, and ground signals which were to be sent to the planes when they came over. Every reception party was provided with a wireless and food – and then there was nothing to do but wait.

We never had an opportunity of thanking in person those fellows who came over on moonlight nights. They gave us what we needed to support life. They gave us arms and equipment to take up the fight afresh, and they had from the very first given us something else that we needed – a feeling of community with all the other soldiers in the war. Those great heavy planes were the link between us and the free world.

The boys' eyes gleamed when the well-known drone of the powerful engines was heard among the mountain walls.

'Do you think they'll come to-night?' was the usual question the new men asked.

The old hands consoled them.

'It's harder work than you think, you booby! The landing-ground has to be cleared in no time. Fifteen or twenty tons to be shifted – that takes some doing!'

And the aircraft came and went. Sometimes they stayed away. Once we spent a fortnight looking for a supply plane which had crashed near one of the bases; but we never found it.

Einar was asked if he would take over the job of preventing enemy sabotage at the Mösvass dam in the event of the Germans withdrawing. The inhabitants of Rjukan lived in well-founded fear that the Germans would blow up the dam, and that the huge masses of water would sweep away a large part of the town. Norsk Hydro set up a special warning service. But if possible we must prevent any devastation being carried out.

Throughout the autumn the weather was unusually bad. It rained unceasingly. Day after day Einar was notified that there would be no drop that night. We had received no food supplies for a year, and gradually all the good things were eaten up.

Tronstad and his party were to come down on Ugleflott, midway between the Kvenna and the Songa. Several times we were warned to be in readiness, and made the long journey in to the landing-ground. A spot far into the mountains had been chosen so that we might be sure of getting the boys down without being detected. It was, too, one of the very few places on the Hardanger Vidda which were suitable for dropping men by parachute.

I was once stranded at the landing-ground with a damaged knee. It was at the end of October, and the weather was snowy. I was not fit to walk the twenty miles back to the hut, and had to take shelter under a large boulder. I lay there with a small wireless set for five days, waiting for the boys to come. I hoped to be able to shoot deer in order to get a little food. Of course none came. On the sixth day I was well enough to go back to Skriubu hut.

We gradually began to wonder whether the boys were really coming. Then I got a telegram telling me to go westwards and wait to receive two men; I was not told who they were, but I expected that Tor Vinje would be one of them.

I started off with Tor Bö as quickly as I could, and reached Bamsebu hut, where Niels Krohg was living by himself. Then all three of us went on to Langesæ to wait for the boys.

The snow had begun falling in October. Knut Haukeliseter and I went on a trip to Vivik, knowing it was the time to catch trout, which were quite thick in the river. We took between sixty and ninety pounds at night in four nets. But it was hard work. When we hauled in the nets, they were stiff with ice directly they came in contact with the air. When we wanted to set them, we had to dip them in water and keep them there so that they should not freeze into a lump. We were always wet, and we were always cold. The snow blizzards blew right into the wretched little hut, and we were short of wood. But we got fish.

The mountains have a special charm in autumn, after the snow has come. They are lonely and desolate. The holiday tourists who in summer have enjoyed the warm sunny slopes and silent tarns would scarcely be able to support life for many days in autumn. All the vegetation seems dead. Nothing is to be seen but driving snow and black rock; the green slopes are gone. The tarns and lakes which in summer are blue and shining are black and forbidding. The snow is whiter and cleaner in autumn than at any other time. Black and white are the only colours the mountains still possess. The days are short and grey, and there are constant gales.

After three days we had hauled up as much fish as we could carry. Movement in the mountains at that time is always exhausting; the snow impedes one's footsteps but is not deep enough for skis. In the semi-darkness one may at any moment be lost in a snow blizzard. The road is many times as long as the winter track; for one has to go round all the lakes and tarns instead of over them.

The journey to Langesæ was tiring, but at least we were not now short of food. There was fish and meat every other day for a long time to come. If only the boys had been able to come with some tobacco! We smoked fag-ends and dirt scraped out of our pipes.

On 17th November the signals came from England: they were to come that night. I went for a long walk to a meat dump which we kept at a place out in the mountains. The boys must have reindeer steak when they arrived in Norway. A short time before I had shot two deer and buried them in the snow. Stomach and intestines had been removed, but I left the skin on. If one goes out shooting in really cold weather the meat will freeze even if the skin is on it, and if a thaw should set in the skin will prevent the meat from thawing as quickly as it would otherwise. Now it was still cold, -5 degrees to -15 degrees F., and the beasts were as stiff as wood. Skinning them was a cold job. The skin was frozen hard to the meat, and I tore it off in small flakes with my bare hands. Now, I thought, the boys were sitting over in England drinking hot tea while they waited for the plane to take off. When my hands grew quite stiff I ran about and beat them on my chest. When at last the blood flowed back into my stiff-frozen fingers the pain was agonising.

'Hell! Damn the reindeer and damn the cold!'

But the boys must have meat. It is the mountain people's custom to offer their guests the best the house can give.

On 18th November two men jumped on to the 'Trond' landing-ground close to the Langesæ hut. They were Tor Vinje and Erling Vestre. For the first time that winter there was a good surface, and they made an easy, soft landing. They had with them arms, first-class equipment, food, coffee and tobacco – and they brought fresh instructions from London.

Erling also brought a complete set of baby clothes for the telegraphist Niels. Niels had had two children during the time he was operating, and his wife lacked clothing for the younger one. Niels telegraphed to England. All good things come from above.

While Erling still hung in the air he called out: 'I've brought your baby clothes.'

We were much amused to find nappies and rompers among arms and explosives.

Erling sketched a new plan for establishing bases for

fugitives who could not get to Sweden. We were to find the men a safe refuge in the mountains and train them for their work when the time came to throw the Germans out. Equipment and food would be provided by the British. It sounded pretty mad at first: our carefully protected security would be entirely lost. We could not live in the mountains in parties of any size without the peasants down in the inhabited areas finding out about us.

Erling was to go west to Suldal and establish a base there. He told us that several of the Linge boys had already landed down on the Fyresdal moors with the same task.

The work with the home forces in the district went ahead more and more rapidly. The platoon commanders were notified that they could get the section commanders together and begin to instruct them. New landing-grounds for parachute drops were being established all the time, and supplies continued to stream in in undreamed of quantities; on some nights so many planes and so much equipment might arrive that we had difficulty in receiving the things. At the New Year of 1945 it was clear that the defeat of the Germans was only a question of time.

Tronstad and his men had come to collect their identity cards from Einar in the mountains to the eastward. Having heard the special prearranged message on the wireless, I went off to meet and have a talk with them.

Tronstad and several of the boys were staying with Einar at Skriubu, which they had made their headquarters for the time being. In particular, I had looked forward to meeting Arne, but unfortunately he had already gone over to Kongsberg, where he was to work as a local commander under Tronstad.

Tronstad's district and mine marched with each other, and we had a number of practical questions to discuss. He wanted some help from Ytre Vinje in the event of any fighting for the Mösvass dam. I wished the area round the Songevatn to be reserved as a possible base for refugees.

It was a busy winter. The section commanders were ordered to assemble their sections and begin training. New contacts were established, and it was decided to call in all the district commanders for commanders' courses in the mountains. To meet all the new demands which now arose I needed more men. Luckily we succeeded in finding some young lads in western Telemark who had been trained to exercise command.

We had difficulties in Suldal. Two of the old contacts there were arrested, and for safety's sake I had to take Knut Rabba from Röldal into the mountains. He was one of the best men for mountain work that I have ever come across.

It became a busy time. All platoon commanders were given permission to call up their men and to begin training. The commanders' courses were held in the mountains east of Suldal, north of Bykle and south of Vinge. It was just the same area which the Germans, two years earlier in the order for their big sweep, had designated as suitable for 'enemy agents.' It was incredible how the fighting capability of the units increased. We could now mobilise three infantry companies and a small staff company. Every single Milorg man had, by March, learned to use his weapons.

I sent a long report to England via Sweden and some extracts may be quoted: 'The training possibilities in the district are very good. We have been able to shoot and test all weapons received. From now on, all men will have their personal weapons at home.' It was really unbelievable what we could do in an occupied country. The Germans at this time had 250,000 men in Norway.

The peasants had always treasured their personal freedom, and they gave solid support to the resistance movement. It was touching to see the pleasure with which we were received in the homesteads all over the countryside. People seemed to forget altogether that receiving us exposed them to great danger.

One day when I met Einar in a farmhouse in Ytre Vinje he had disturbing news for me. Lognvik, the local magistrate in Rauland, had observed that illegal work was being carried on in the district. Syverstad had been to see him, laid his pistol on the table and said that if the magistrate valued his life he must hold his tongue. Lognvik had promised to do this. But now it had been discovered that he had tried to get into touch with the Gestapo at Rjukan to tell them what he knew. It was decided to shoot him.

I did not like this business at all. Rauland lay on the borders of my district, and an affair of the kind would always lead to German investigations and a great deal of talk.

On the morning of 12th March, while I was in Ytre Vinje, a man came over from Rauland and told me that Lognvik had been shot during the night. I got in touch with the boys immediately and ordered that all movements and operations in the district should stop at once, and that all who felt themselves threatened should leave their homes. The messenger, Sveinung Olsnes, was sent to his home on the borders of Rauland to obtain all the latest news. The warning system was notified and held in readiness for immediate action.

These measures were soon proved to have been necessary when it was reported that German cars were moving westwards from Seljord. Our warning service enabled us to follow them across the countryside – big covered lorries containing an unknown number of troops. They passed through Vinje about noon on their way to Rauland.

Sveinung came back from Rauland and told us that two men had arrived at Olsnes quite worn out. They had asked for Bonzo or Knut and begged that the following message might be sent:

'Julius and Kaare shot last night in an encounter with magistrate Lognvik and his brother.'

Julius was Tronstad's cover name and Kaare was Syverstad's. It was not the magistrate, then, who had been shot the night before. Now there would be the devil to pay.

Soon afterwards a message came saying that the young men of Rauland had mobilised and assembled at Arabygdi, right in the heart of Totak – the most northerly inhabited area of the Rauland country. We were also informed that Einar had gone off on a trip to the eastward.

I was at my wits' end. The situation had become more acute than it had been for a long time. German troops were in Rauland, and the Rauland men were fully mobilised: a collision might be expected at any time. What made the business so much more serious was that the boys had no responsible leader. If there was fighting, the Germans would most certainly make short work of the untrained Milorg men. We must act, and act quickly. I got hold of a couple of sten guns from the nearest dump and, as soon as it began to grow dark, moved off northwards to find Niels Krohg. He was at Bögrend with his wife, who was just expecting a child.

Niels had already heard about the German troop movements when I arrived, but not about Tronstad and Syverstad. As we sat there talking a bus came down the road and stopped outside Tor Bö's house. What could this mean?

Niels and I dashed out, each grabbing a sten gun, and ran into the wood. Had things gone so far that the Germans had begun to take the boys one by one? Suddenly I caught sight of a man crossing the road, and stopped him. It was Tor Vinje. He told me that one of the Rauland men had arrived at our uppermost warning station at the village post-office in Edland. The man brought a message of greeting from Einar and was going to try to find me. From the post office they had informed Vaagslid, and Vaagslid had been in touch with Tor, who lived about ten miles away. Tor had stolen a bus and come down to find me. He had met the Rauland man at the post office and brought him along in the bus. Einar wanted help, the man said.

We turned the bus round and drove up the Haukeli road, making plans as we went. The Rauland men must clear out, and clear out quickly. If there was any kind of a brush between the Milorg forces and the Germans in Rauland, it might be the spark which set light to the powder barrel. So the boys must go, but where and how? We had fairly large food supplies at our western base, but we were short, and more than short, of housing accommodation. At a pinch we might put up thirty or forty men if we used all the huts between Vaagslid and Suldal.

We parked the bus at the side of the road a short way up towards Grungedal. Niels went off to disperse the commanders at once. It was a pity to have to interrupt the lads' training four days after they had begun, and after the long preparations; but this business was more important. Niels also carried with him a telegram to London which ran as follows:

'Deeply regret to have to inform you that the Professor and Kaare have been killed according to a report from Rauland. German troops are in Rauland and the whole organisation and others have taken to the hills. Leaving to-night for the upper inhabited areas in Rauland to try to collect the Milorg boys and take them to a safe place. Have taken all security measures in my district. Will give all the help I can.'

With Tor and the Rauland man I took the track over the mountains to Arabygdi. We arrived in the morning and found armed Rauland men at every single farm. They told us that they had a guard out on the ice. I had a messenger sent to fetch Björn Gardsjord, who was the responsible platoon commander in Rauland. He came with Jon Landsverk, who had been present when Tronstad and Syverstad were shot.

Jon told us that he had fetched the magistrate Lognvik, telling him that a hut had been broken into and that he ought to look into the matter. Then, on the way, Lognvik was taken prisoner by Tronstad and Syverstad. They went into a hut by the Syrtebekk in the neighbourhood of the Mösvatn. This consisted of two rooms, and they sat in the inner one.

Tronstad was in uniform and interrogated Lognvik to find out what plans the N.S. had in the event of an invasion. It was decided to keep the magistrate a prisoner at a place in Kvendalen till the war was over. Syverstad sat with his pistol on his knees.

Suddenly Jon caught sight of a hand, holding a pistol, appearing round the door which led to the other room. A series of shots rang out, and he knew nothing more of what happened. He thought, however, that Syverstad must have fallen at once, and that Tronstad had dashed into the other room; several shots had come from there. Lognvik had jumped up, grabbed a carbine which was standing against the wall, and disappeared.

When Jon had come to himself again, Syverstad was lying on the floor. He was shot through the head, but was still breathing. Tronstad was lying in the outer room. He too was shot through the head, and was dead.

Jon ran out and got hold of Einar, who was at Neset Farm, by the Mösvatn. They went back together and found the hut just as Jon had left it. Jon covered Einar while he was inside clearing away papers and other things which ought to be saved. They got hold of a sledge, carried the bodies out and sunk them in a hole in the ice of a tarn hard by. All was now quiet.

Then Einar gave orders for the mobilisation of the whole

Rauland platoon, to capture the two men before they could get in touch with the Germans. He and Jon thought the man who had fired must have been Lognvik's brother. Guards were posted between the Syrtebekk and the village, and a watch was kept on Lognvik Farm. But the magistrate and his brother could not be taken.

When day began to break, Einar sent all the Rauland men along the ice of the Totakvatn to assemble at Arabygdi. He asked Jon Landsverk and the platoon commander Björn Gardsjord to get in touch with me so that I might help them. Einar himself went off eastwards to find Jens, who would be in command of the group now that Tronstad was dead.

The 'Sunshine' group had lost its leader when Professor Tronstad was killed. But Norway had lost one of the best men she had during her war of liberation.

The situation was precarious. The Germans had a detachment at Rauland, only two and a half miles away along the Totakvatn. We did not know how strong they were, but we knew that they had already put patrols out over the mountains. A German patrol had been observed earlier in the day on the ice off Arabygdi. If it came to a fight, the badly organised and almost untrained home forces would undoubtedly come off worst. The hamlets would probably be burnt down and the mountain-dwellers exposed to the horrors of war in earnest.

For two years we had been doing our utmost to carry out our work in such a way as not to involve our friends in danger and disaster. Were they not to be spared after all?

The mobilised Milorg forces must be got away, and got away quickly. Every trace of us must be covered up, all connections with the inhabited areas must be broken, and the slate wiped clean.

Gardsjord called the section commanders together, and I gave orders that the boys should be assembled within two hours and marched off to an unknown destination. They were to meet by sections outside the farm where we were. I distributed all the money I had between four men and ordered them to buy as much food as they could from the farms.

The men were ready at three and we were able to start. We succeeded in getting the march organised by sections, with the men in single file and properly spaced out. There were four sections, each of about ten men. The best hillmen were in the section from Arabygdi. They were ordered to retire to the area round the Songevatn, whence they were to renew contact with Rauland and report every German movement to Vaagslid. In no circumstances were they to fight, and, if it were found necessary, they were to retire across the Songedal. They would find huts at the head of the valley which were not marked on the map.

The rest of us made off westwards. There was a ringing hard crust on the snow, and we left no tracks. After a two days' march, Tor Vinje and I, with thirty weary Rauland men, came over to the south side of the Haukeli road.

The Rauland men remained with us in the west till conditions in their own district became quieter. I got into touch with Einar and Jens through London and informed them that the men were safe – and at their disposal whenever they might need them.

Conditions in the camp were difficult. In the first place there was little space. As many as twenty men were quartered in a hut in which there was ordinarily room for only eight. We had no wood in the area; and this had to be fetched from a long way off. Food had to be obtained. London promised us clothes, boots, sleeping-bags, tents and food; but the weather was consistently bad, and the supplies did not come. Luckily at that time there were plenty of reindeer round about, and shoots on a big scale were set on foot. We had stored some food from previous drops, so that we managed quite well.

Our communications with the inhabited areas were first class. The food officer in Vinje placed 4,500 lbs. of flour at our disposal. This was done after a conference with one of the members of the food council. I said that I needed the flour and had full powers from London to requisition it if necessary. Both food and clothing came from Rauland. No one there knew the whereabouts of the men they were helping, but they collected butter, and the shops sent bread and tobacco. When the people in the mountain villages realised that matters were serious, there was no limit to what we could get. In certain hamlets in Vinje the women had been putting aside butter and woollen garments all through the winter with a view to possible fighting.

Many of the Raulanders were not accustomed to living in the mountains in winter in such difficult conditions. We had good and bad days in turn, but my own general impression was that we had bad weather at the time when we so sorely needed sun and warmth. Still, the high morale of our home forces enabled them to overcome most of the difficulties.

London arranged a meeting between Jens, Einar and myself, at which we discussed the conditions that would arise in the event of fighting, or of a German capitulation. According to existing plans it was the task of the Rauland troop to see that the Mösvass dam was not blown up by the Germans. It was now decided that the Rauland men should hold themselves in readiness to seize the dam. This meant that they must be trained as effective soldiers, and must be good enough to go into action against German troops.

The men gradually became efficient enough to operate in detachments. But housing conditions in the camp were so bad that we were continually discussing the possibility of moving. At the beginning of April we transferred the whole camp eastwards to the Songevatn, where an area had been reconnoitred which could take 220 men if necessary.

At the Songevatn we had good accommodation, and the situation had become so quiet that it was possible to continue the commanders' courses. The company, platoon and section commanders in Vinje were assembled again. Along with the Rauland men, who belonged to the neighbouring district, they received very good military instruction.

It was clear that the end of the war was approaching, though we did not know how the situation in Norway would develop. It was quite possible that the Germans would be desperate enough to continue the struggle in *Festung Norwegen* after Germany had fallen. If anything of the kind should happen, the first requirement would be that there should be forces in Norway sufficiently strong and well-armed to prevent really serious devastation by the Germans. England kept on sending us larger and larger consignments of arms, and by degrees we got so much that we had more equipment than we could mobilise men to use.

The camp by the Songevatn, therefore, became of increasing importance. The commanders of the home forces could obtain there the training and instruction they needed to be able to go home and continue their work in the villages round about. We had a sufficient number of previously trained commanders to form a staff and keep the camp going.

A curious life developed round the Songevatn. We had 'fenced off' a large area of the Hardanger Vidda inside the German closed area. The training was carried out as on a regular training ground. An exact programme was arranged, and orders of the day issued in writing. But the men under training showed an interest which I am sure is seldom displayed at any regular Norwegian establishment. To make the boys efficient as soon as possible live ammunition was used in all exercises, and a great deal of explosive was consumed.

We put all the tracks leading in towards our area in a state of defence to prevent small enemy forces from approaching. If we had been attacked, we should have avoided an engagement as long as possible. But we were now over a hundred strong, and the time was past when single Gestapo agents could terrorise us in the high mountains. The thought that continually tormented us was how we could prevent any fighting that might develop from having consequences on the inhabited areas.

Food supply, and quartermaster's work as a whole, became a regular organisation in itself. The camp required many hundreds of pounds of food daily, sometimes more than fifty loaves. We had a number of horses, which were at work every single day.

Now, as before, the reindeer saved the situation. Our shooting parties were out daily and obtained huge supplies of reindeer meat. The only kind of food which was not rationed in the camp was meat. On one occasion the quartermaster reported that the boys had eaten thirty-two reindeer in twelve days.

In this last stage of the war the Germans began to be aggressive. They carried out a number of sweeps in Upper Telemark, and several of our people were arrested. But in every case we were able to isolate the enemy parties, so that they could not come any farther.

At Rjukan the resistance gradually became very efficient. The Germans had a couple of heavy anti-aircraft batteries on the top of the mountain, at the terminus of the cable railway which normally carried people up to the mountains from the valley. One day, through carelessness on their own part, they had an explosion in an ammunition dump up there, and the terminus of the cable railway collapsed. Now that there was no more heavy water to be protected, the anti-aircraft batteries were to be moved. The guns and ammunition were taken down by the same narrow path we had used to get into the mountains after the attack on Vemork two years before. The ammunition was driven by horse and sledge – by Norwegians.

Every day our fellows kicked a few shells out of the sledges into the snow. Every night these shells were collected, opened in the Hydro's workshops and filled with a very high explosive instead of the usual type. Then, next day, they were mixed up with the other shells.

The shells were sent on and spread among the German anti-aircraft defences all over Norway. When the R.A.F. attacked the German naval station at Horten the anti-aircraft fire suddenly ceased – one or two of the guns had burst and killed or wounded their crews.

Knut Rabba got into difficulties in Röldal. He had been in the mountains for several months and had been trained; then he had gone home again. One night the Germans came to arrest him. He had learnt one thing from us – to sleep with a pistol on the table by his bed – and that saved him. He jumped out of the window in his stockings, with his shoes in one hand, and shot his way to freedom. Just as Knut had got through a patch of wood and over some boulders and up on to a slight eminence a short way from the village, a whole troop of Germans rushed across a field just below him. They had no idea what a good reindeer-hunter they were up against and what danger they themselves were in. But Knut, like all other commanders in the home forces, had received strict orders not to fight Germans except to save himself or his comrades. So good was his discipline that he let the Germans fire at him at two hundred yards' range – but when he himself was in a good position up on a hill-top he refrained from firing at them when they came running in a crowd across the field below.

The Germans came to Vaagslid on one of the first days of May, and asked for me. For the first time in the war they had somehow found out that I was in the country. But now it was too late.

The inhabitants of Vaagslid retired into the mountains under the protection of the company which was stationed by the Songevatn. The Germans did indeed feel their way in with single patrols, but we left them in peace. Nothing was to be gained by starting a fight now.

On 8th May we were notified from London that we could come out into the open. The few German troops which were in the district were interned in their camps after a short telephone message to the commandant. The home forces took over all control. The long working day was over.

10. THE FIGHT FOR HEAVY WATER

Now and then people have asked me why we fought in the war. That is a question we never really asked ourselves. It was a matter of course that we should fight. It is impossible to say in every case whether our boys' reaction to events was due to what from time immemorial has been called patriotism, or, as some think, to a desire for adventure.

I should say, however, that only in very few cases was it a desire for adventure that impelled them to take up arms against the foreign invaders. There is little that is adventurous about war, and the boys had small chance of satisfying a desire for adventure in a war in which toil and hunger, and the idea of death at the hands of a firing-squad, were our daily companions. We lost many of our best comrades, not only in battle but also as helpless victims in the hands of the Gestapo.

Most of the lads I met during the war gave, I am sure, little thought to the question. They felt quite simply that our country and our people were worth fighting for. For many it was perhaps easier to fight than to let things be.

We gradually came to understand that one's fatherland is not only scenery and ancient history; it is first and foremost the society in which one lives. What counted was not where or how we lived, but that we were Norwegian, and were holding our little bit of the front.

In May, 1945, the most curious army our country has ever seen appeared in the light of day. About 57,000 men of the Norwegian home forces took over control and authority throughout the country. They were nearly all young lads, who for several years had been training and preparing for the day when they would be able to strike a blow for their faith and their people.

This army is all the more curious in that it was a hundred-per-cent volunteer force; not one man had been called up to serve against his will. For several years it had been their daily lot to give ground, and go on giving ground, in the face of German encroachments, while man after man was taken and disappeared. Now they came forth in a body.

A people which can mobilise 57,000 men in such conditions should always be able to exist as a free people.

The Norwegian home forces were established primarily to be able to fight the foreign invaders on Norwegian soil. The Allies undertook to supply them. Norwegian detachments in England and in Sweden undertook to train them, and sent instructors and commanders.

These groups played a part too in the war seen as a whole. They tied down large German forces in Norway, and in the last six months of the war prevented the Germans from withdrawing southwards. They blew up roads, bridges, ships, and railways. They obtained for the Allies regular and accurate information about enemy dispositions and movements. And they kept the spirit of resistance alive in the people.

One of the greatest tasks the home forces undertook was to stop the German production of heavy water in Norway.

Heavy water was of interest to scientific research workers at quite an early date, but only small quantities of it were required. During the war this curious liquid acquired a new and terrible significance.

A war is decided first and foremost by good weapons. Good weapons are instruments with great killing power. When scientists had once discovered that there was a possibility of splitting atoms and releasing energy, the idea of making use of this process to evolve a weapon – the most terrible the world had ever seen – was not far away.

When the Germans occupied Norway, they immediately became interested in the manufacture of heavy water at Rjukan. The Allies were working at high pressure on experiments for the making of an atom bomb, and were desperately afraid of the Germans getting in ahead of them.

Norwegian home forces gave the Allies exact information about the manufacture of heavy water at Vemork during the war. Norwegian scientists and engineers came to England and made their information and their abilities available in the fight against the most fearful of the secret weapons.

On the military side, in the struggle, the British first tried to stop the Vemork factory by using regular commando troops with gliders. This failed. Then the Gunnerside group was formed, and sabotage proved successful.

In the autumn of 1943 there was again the danger of the Germans accumulating enough heavy water for their atomic piles, so the Americans employed their vast strength in bombing Rjukan. Professor Tronstad had tried all along to prevent bombing, and the results showed that he was right; the use of aircraft on a large scale had comparatively little effect, but it forced the Germans to move the production to Germany.

The ferry had to be sunk in the Tinnsjö to complete the job. For the third time men's lives were lost in the struggle for the precious drops. But once again, sabotage was successful.

EPILOGUE

The German scientist, Otto Hahn, had already established in 1938-9 at the Kaiser Wilhelm Institute in Berlin, the fission of uranium. This discovery led logically to the idea of making an atomic explosive for use in war, based upon the uranium isotope 235.

The Germans quickly called their first conference of scientists in April, 1939 and by the end of the year they had concluded that uranium with heavy water or graphite as a moderator would produce a great amount of energy in an atomic pile. In August of the same year, the now famous letter was written from Einstein to President Roosevelt warning him about the possibilities of atomic explosives.

The race was on.

In the middle of 1940, both the Germans and the Allies became aware of 'the plutonium alternative'. The artificial element, plutonium, can be produced in any atomic pile based upon uranium. This is the other atomic explosive. This was unquestionably an easier way to make an atomic bomb than to separate the isotope 235 from ordinary uranium.

For the 'Manhattan Project' in the U.S.A. they chose both ways. The bomb on Hiroshima was a uranium bomb. The bomb over Nagasaki was a plutonium bomb.

In Germany the scientists first of all concentrated on building an atomic pile. They had their uranium in Czechoslovakia or from stocks in Belgium. They needed heavy water from Norway or very pure graphite. Now one of the coincidences of history took place. They found that graphite would not work. The Germans needed five tons of heavy water from Vemork in Norway to make an atomic pile produce.

This is no school book on nuclear physics, and indeed the author is not qualified for this. The book is a report on Norwegian resistance faced with the possibility of a Nazi victory in the last war.

Hundreds of Norwegian women and men took a direct or indirect part in this struggle. Most of them never knew what was at stake; but their assistance was necessary because it gave us the environment we needed to operate in. They included the local population in Western Telemark, the farmers at Mösvatn Lake, and last but not least, the townspeople of Rjukan itself.

Some German sources have tried to claim long after the war that their scientists were unwilling to give Adolf Hitler the decisive weapon in his war upon mankind. It is owed to everyone who took part in this fight, and those who gave their lives, and the next of kin, to write this short epilogue and to examine the claim a little more closely.

Much has been written about the German nuclear effort during the great war of 1939 to 1945. Should this epilogue be inconclusive, it is solely because of the author's inability to find all necessary sources, but the picture has become clear enough to draw some conclusions.

After the experimental groundwork that was done in 1939 up to the middle of 1940, on both sides of the struggle, the Germans concentrated on getting an atomic pile into production. By this process they hoped to get sufficient plutonium to make an atomic bomb. The size of this bomb would, according to their own information given to their military leaders, 'be the size of a pineapple.'

After the theory of uranium fission had been established the way to construct a weapon was only too clear. It only remained to work and experiment. The Germans had scientists of a very high order – this in spite of the fact that they had made some of their best men and women fugitives from their own land because of their Jewish ancestry.

In war-time an extremely close priority is necessary when allotting resources to industry. The decision to go ahead was, therefore, a political one. Until the end of 1942, Adolf Hitler operated on the assumption that he would win the war within a few months with conventional weapons. The scientists at Kaiser Wilhelm Institute worked, therefore, under the handicap of low priorities, made worse because they could never show any results. They were never able to get the minimum amount of heavy water accumulated to make their pile produce. For this they needed 5,000 kilograms of the precious liquid – Vemork never gave them more than about 2,600 kilograms as a total.

By the end of 1942, the Germans had lost the initiative in the war; and they struggled desperately to fill the ever-growing requirements for conventional weapons. At this time the allied bombing offensive got into its stride and scientific and industrial research was getting more and more difficult in Germany. By the end of 1943, the Germans were beginning to lose the possibility of even giving priority.

The author has found a German report which is part of a book *Deutsche Geheimwaffen* (German secret weapons) written by Fritz Hahn. From this report I quote:

'Another insoluble problem was the supply of D_2O (heavy water). With the occupation of Norway the only factory in Europe producing D_2O fell into German hands. The production before the war was about 10 litres per month, but nearly all stocks had been removed to England. Within a year production was brought up to 120 litres per month and in 1940 even up to 300 litres. On 28th February, 1943, the plant was blown up by a Norwegian Commando group which had landed by parachute. Some stocks were destroyed and in addition there was a loss of two months' production.

'In spite of the decision on 6th June, 1942, to stop all experiments on a possible atom bomb, Hitler and Himmler, because of the deteriorating position on the front, now inconsistently demanded such a weapon.

'First of all it was decided to bring all apparatus to Germany to set up a plant in Austria for the production of D_2O, but a ferry bringing this plant and the D_2O to Germany was sunk on Tinnsjö Lake by a Norwegian resistance member by means of a time bomb. Nothing was saved from the boat.[1] The Kaiser Wilhelm Institute had at this time 1,370 litres in stock. To build a new factory was now impossible because of the time involved and at several places it was attempted to build small experimental plants for the production of D_2O.'

Fritz Hahn also mentioned other reasons for the failure in making an atomic bomb in Germany; the lack of large cyclotrons; the lack of very pure uranium oxide; and Hitler's indecision at the early stage of the war.

In the fall of 1944 the high concentration plant at Vemork was dismantled and sent to Germany. It was found in the

1. Wrong: four drums with the equivalent of 121 litres floated up and were salvaged.

village of Hechtingen in Bavaria on 22nd April, by English and American intelligence officers.

An atomic pile was also found in Haigerlock in Bavaria with uranium and heavy water that was on the brink of going critical. It lacked about 700 litres of additional heavy water.

Of all the 'buts' and 'ifs' which follow all historical discussions, none are so unstable and encumbered with variable values as those which come as an aftermath of war. One seldom finds one cause for one effect. History is not a chain where one joint necessarily gives a continuity of units to the next joint. One cannot therefore, by breaking one joint, make the whole chain useless. If Adolf Hitler's failure in producing the decisive weapon of the Second World War was due to lack of foresight, lack of proficiency, lack of willingness by his scientists, lack of freedom of research, or lack of heavy water, it is in this connection a matter of little consequence. The final result was that it failed. A later inquiry will always find itself on the borderline between 'can' and 'wish' and will tend strongly towards the most attractive conclusion.

The mass slaughter which resulted from the uranium bomb over Hiroshima and the plutonium bomb over Nagasaki could even on the last war's scale, scare everyone. The resulting atompsychosis based upon radioactive downfall over mother earth has left a shaken humanity. The scientists all over the world, on the allied side as well, have, whenever possible, disclaimed their part in the production of the bomb. When a war is going on there is no free exchange of ideas across the front lines, and the political leadership has a tremendous responsibility. Everyone can imagine what an atomic weapon in Adolf Hitler's hands would have led to.

It was under this threat that the allied governments gave their soldiers and scientists their means and their orders.